The Communist Postscript

The Communist Postscript

BORIS GROYS

Translated by Thomas H. Ford

VERSO
London • New York

This paperback edition first published by Verso 2022
First published by Verso 2009
Translation © Thomas H. Ford 2009, 2022
Foreword © Thomas H. Ford 2009, 2022
First published as *Das kommunistische Postskriptum*
© Suhrkamp Verlag GmbH und Co. KG 2006
All rights reserved

1 3 5 7 9 10 8 6 4 2

Verso
UK: 6 Meard Street, London W1F 0EG
US: 388 Atlantic Avenue, Brooklyn, NY 11217
versobooks.com

Verso is the imprint of New Left Books

ISBN-13: 978-1-84467-432-9
ISBN-13: 978-1-78478-030-2 (US EBK)
ISBN-13: 978-1-78478-029-6 (UK EBK)

British Library Cataloguing in Publication Data
A catalogue record for this book is available from the British Library

Library of Congress Cataloging-in-Publication Data
A catalog record for this book is available from the Library of Congress

Typeset by Hewer Text UK Ltd, Edinburgh
Printed and bound by CPI Group (UK) Ltd, Croydon CR0 4YY

Contents

Translator's Foreword

First published in German in 2006, Boris Groys's *The Communist Postscript* is both a revision of standard accounts of the history of the Soviet Union and a philosophical renewal of the idea of communism. It is also a postcommunist manifesto: Groys's short text can be read as forming a bookend to the modern experience of communism heralded by *The Communist Manifesto*. Sharing much of the rhetorical clarity and polemical brio of Marx and Engels's *Manifesto*, *The Communist Postscript* stands in little need of any explanatory preface. While Groys's arguments are politically challenging and theoretically complex, they are constructed in such a way as to present readers with few obstacles to initial comprehension. Nonetheless, because this is a philosophical book about communism, there are certain difficulties inherent in translating it into English that need to be acknowledged.

These problems arise not because English is in effect the hegemonic language of capitalism today. As Groys argues, capitalist economic processes are not linguistic: capitalism does not in fact speak English, nor any other language. Yet

English, perhaps more than many other languages, may be said to have accepted and internalized the subordinate social function of language under capitalism. English in many cases advertises what in other languages is veiled using more traditional means of ideological obfuscation. In exile in America during the war, Brecht commented in his journal on the use of the word 'sell' to mean persuade, as in the sentence 'the task facing the President is that of selling the war to the people.' In Brecht's unfinished *Refugee Conversations*, this observation is further developed by the character Ziffel, as suggesting that in America, more than elsewhere, ideas are recognized to be commodities. In America, he states, in discussions of scientific or aesthetic problems, one says 'I buy that' in order to express agreement. This proximity of concepts to the commodity form can also be tracked in Anglophone philosophy over the last century. For example, it was in order to draw a distinction between continental philosophy and philosophy in English that William James introduced the metaphor of 'cash-value' – of 'cashing' an idea in experience as a way to test its meaningfulness. This metaphor has subsequently become generally accepted in Anglo-American philosophy, embedding reference to market value in arguments about topics that may at first glance appear to be quite remote from commercial concerns.

The Communist Postscript suggests that these and other similar figures of language are far less metaphoric than is often thought. Under capitalist conditions, Groys argues, the significance of a concept is indeed primarily measured in terms of its value in the marketplace. And by frequently using English expressions – killer instinct; Batman forever; agreement to disagree; win-win; anything goes; race, class and gender – to mark moments of strategic irony in his text, Groys acknowledges the expressive openness of the contemporary English language to its own commodification. If, in these ways, English indeed avows its enrolment in the assault of market values against other potential sources of social meaning and forms of social organization, then a brief account of the specifically German context of a few of Groys's key terms may be justified.

Central to Groys's understanding of communism is his notion of the 'linguistification' of society. The German word here is *Versprachlichung*, a term principally employed in sociology, and formed from the verb *versprachlichen*, which means 'to verbalize' or 'put into words'. But the 'verbalization of society' does not capture Groys's meaning. Linguistification as used here does not mean to provide a verbal description of society, but rather to organize and shape society using language. Rather than merely putting non-linguistic social relations and processes into words so as to describe them, linguistification involves their total transformation into language. Probably the best-known prior use of 'linguistification' to translate *Versprachlichung* in this sense occurs in the section 'The Linguistification of the Sacred' in the English edition of Jürgen Habermas's *Theory of Communicative Action*. As for Habermas, linguistification for Groys entails that social practices and beliefs become open to discursive criticism and challenge. But the linguistification central to communism in Groys's account encompasses a much greater range of social existence than is at issue for Habermas. Partly in consequence, while Habermas's notion of communicative action remains oriented towards a horizon of ultimate consensus, linguistification for Groys exacerbates social divisions and contradictions.

Groys makes frequent use of the term *Evidenz*. This is not a straightforward equivalent of the English 'evidence', either in everyday language or in philosophical discourse. The predominant philosophical use of 'evidence' in English is relatively continuous with its use in legal and scientific contexts: evidence is understood as the currency in which a proposition may be verified, corroborated or empirically 'cashed'. It refers to the relevant phenomena that justify advancing a hypothesis as true. Groys's sense remains closer to the German philosophical tradition, in which *Evidenz* refers more to an immanent quality of judgement and knowledge than to the external means of deriving and supporting conclusions. In other words, *Evidenz* primarily describes what is rationally evident, rather than that which is evidence of or for something; Kant, for example, defines *Evidenz* as 'intuitive certainty' in the *Critique of Pure Reason*. *Evidenz* has been translated here simply as 'evidence', rather than by other approximations to the German sense such as 'self-evidence' or 'certainty.' This German context should be kept in mind, however. The phrase 'the effulgence of evidence', for instance, does not refer to a surfeit of corroborating material, but to the illuminating force of conviction that legitimates judgements.

Groys most frequently uses *Evidenz* in this sense to describe the force of conviction communicated when an argument previously taken to be logically valid is revealed to contain a paradox. The conviction in question is therefore predominantly critical: the evidence is that of a paradox, rather than that of a proof. The logic of paradox outlined by Groys is one that proliferates divisions, a logic committed to sparking contradiction and internal contestation. Groys contrasts this paradoxical logic to the logical regime, often presumed central to Western philosophy, that is constituted by principles such as those of non-contradiction and the excluded middle. His shorthand designation for this logic of non-contradiction is 'formal logic', and he frequently uses this in adjectival form in phrases such as 'formal-logical validity'. Rather than resorting to circuitous paraphrases, I have retained this doubled adjective, formal-logical, despite its slight awkwardness in English.

Groys writes that communism is the transcription of society into the medium of language. The construction of communism could be understood in this sense as an act of translation carried to its utmost extremity, an exercise of hitherto unparalleled translinguistic energies. Like that world-shaking transcriptive enterprise, communism, even translations such as this one are by necessity collective undertakings, and I would like to express my gratitude to Boris Groys for his generous help in reading through the manuscript and suggesting improvements, and to the many others who provided assistance and advice.

Introduction

The subject of this book is communism. How one speaks about communism depends on what one takes communism to mean. In what follows, I will understand communism to be the project of subordinating the economy to politics in order to allow politics to act freely and sovereignly. The economy functions in the medium of money. It operates with numbers. Politics functions in the medium of language. It operates with words – with arguments, programmes and petitions, but also with commands, prohibitions, resolutions and decrees. The communist revolution is the transcription of society from the medium of money to the medium of language. It is a linguistic turn at the level of social praxis. Thus it is not enough to define man as a speaking being, as is generally done in modern philosophy, notwithstanding all the subtleties and differences that distinguish one individual philosophical position from another. So long as humans live under the conditions of the capitalist economy they remain fundamentally mute because their fate does not speak to them. If a human is not addressed by his or her fate, then he or she is also incapable of answering it. Economic processes are anonymous, and not expressed in words. For this reason one cannot enter into discussion with economic processes; one cannot change their mind, convince them, persuade them, use words to win them over to one's side. All that can be done is to adapt one's own behaviour to what is occurring. Economic failure brooks no argument, just as economic success requires no additional discursive justification. In capitalism, the ultimate confirmation or refutation of human action is not linguistic but economic: it is expressed not with words but with numbers. The force of language as such is thereby annulled.

Humans will first truly become beings who exist in language and through language only once fate is no longer mute and no longer governs at a purely economic level, but is instead formulated discursively and decided politically from the outset, as is the case in communism. Humans thereby gain the possibility of arguing, protesting and agitating against the decisions of fate. Such arguments and protests may not always prove effective. They may often be ignored or even suppressed, but they are not as such meaningless. It is entirely meaningful and justified to oppose political decisions in the medium of language, because those decisions were themselves reached in the medium of language. Under capitalist conditions, by contrast, every criticism and every protest is fundamentally senseless, for in capitalism language itself functions as a commodity, that is to say, it is inherently mute. Discourses of critique and protest are recognized as successful when they sell well, and to have failed when they sell poorly. Thus in no respect can these discourses be distinguished from other commodities, which are equally silent – or speak only in self-advertisement.

Criticism of capitalism does not operate in the same medium as capitalism itself. In terms of their media, capitalism and its discursive critique are incompatible and so can never encounter each other. Society must first be altered by its linguistification if it is to become subject to any meaningful critique. Thus we can reformulate Marx's famous thesis that philosophy should not interpret the world, but instead change it: for society to become subject to criticism, it must first become communist. This explains the instinctive preference for communism felt by all those equipped with critical consciousness, for only communism performs the total linguistification of human fate that opens the space for a total critique.

Communist society can be defined as one in which power and the critique of power operate in the same medium. If the question is posed, therefore, of whether the regime of the former Soviet Union should be regarded as communist – and this question appears unavoidable whenever communism is discussed today – then, in the light of the definition given above, the answer is yes. The Soviet Union went further towards realizing the communist project historically than any other preceding society. During the 1930s every kind of private property was completely abolished. The political leadership thus gained the possibility of taking decisions that were independent of particular economic interests. But it was not that these particular interests had been suppressed; they simply no longer existed. Every citizen of the Soviet Union worked as an employee of the Soviet state, lived in housing that belonged to the state, shopped in state stores and travelled through the state's territory by means of state-run transport. What economic interests could such a citizen have? Only the interest that affairs of state would improve, so that the citizen of this state would be better able to profit – no matter whether legally or illegally, through work or through corruption. In the Soviet Union, a fundamental identity between private and public interest thus prevailed. The single external constraint was military: the Soviet Union had to defend itself against its external enemies. By the 1960s, however, the military capabilities of the country had become so great that the possibility of belligerent attack from outside could be rated as extremely improbable. From that moment the Soviet leadership stood in no 'objective' conflict: it had no internal opposition, and it was also subject to no external constraints that could limit its administrative powers over the country. Its practical decisions could therefore be guided solely by its independent political reason, its own inner convictions. Granted, this political reason – because it was dialectical reason – led the Soviet leadership to abolish communism of its own free will. Yet this decision in no way alters the fact that communism must be considered to have been realized in the Soviet Union. To the contrary: as will be shown in what follows, it is this decision that makes the realization, the embodiment, the incarnation of communism complete.

In any case it cannot be said that the Soviet Union failed economically, for economic failure is only possible in the market. But the market did not exist in the Soviet Union. Hence neither the economic success nor the economic failure of the political leadership could be established 'objectively', that is to say, neutrally, non-ideologically. Certain commodities were produced in the Soviet Union not because they sold well on the market, but because they conformed to an ideological vision of the communist future. And on the other hand, those commodities that could not be legitimated ideologically were not produced. This was true of all commodities, not just the texts or images of official propaganda. In Soviet communism, every commodity became an ideologically relevant statement, just as in capitalism every statement becomes a commodity. One could eat communistically, house and dress oneself communistically – or likewise non-communistically, or even anti-communistically. This meant that in the Soviet

Union it was in theory just as possible to protest against the shoes or eggs or sausage then available in the stores as it was to protest against the official doctrines of historical materialism. They could be criticized in the same terms because these doctrines had the same original source as the shoes, eggs and sausage – namely, the relevant decisions of the Politburo of the Central Committee of the CPSU. Everything in communist existence was the way it was because someone had said that it should be thus and not otherwise. And everything that is decided in language can be criticized linguistically as well.

The question of whether communism is possible is therefore profoundly connected to the question of whether government, organization and political administration can be carried out in language and through language. This central question can be formulated as follows: can language as such ever exercise sufficient force for society to be governed by linguistic means at all – and if so, under what conditions? This possibility is often flatly denied: in our era especially, the view predominates that language as such has no force at all and is entirely powerless. This assessment accurately reflects the situation of language under capitalist conditions. In capitalism, language is indeed powerless. On the basis of this understanding of language, it is also generally assumed that in communism the ruling apparatuses characteristically acted behind a facade of official language and compelled

people to accept the language of power. And this assumption
is not entirely unjustified. Indeed, this suspicion appears
to be sufficiently confirmed by the long history of political
repression in communist countries.

But this leaves open the question of why these oppressive
apparatuses acted in favour of one particular ideological
conception, and not in favour of some alternative
conception. For the loyalty of these apparatuses with regard
to a particular ideology cannot be taken for granted. To be
loyal and to remain loyal, these apparatuses had first to be
persuaded, to be won over. Otherwise they would remain
immobile and fail to act, as was indeed the case at the end
of the communist states of Eastern Europe. Moreover, under
communist conditions, these apparatuses cannot be cleanly
separated from the rest of society, for in a society which
consists exclusively of state employees – and Soviet society
was such a society – the question about who oppresses
whom, and how, cannot be posed in the same way as it is in
a society in which the apparatuses of power are more or less
cleanly separated from civil society. When state violence
in communist states is considered, it must therefore not
be forgotten that this violence was conveyed through
language – through commands and decrees with which
one might comply, but equally might not. The leaderships
of the communist countries understood this much better
than their opponents did. It was for this reason that these

leaderships invested so much force and energy into shaping and maintaining the language of official ideology and were so incensed by minimal deviations from it. They knew that outside of language they actually possessed nothing – and that if they lost their control over language, they would lose everything.

The theory of Marxism–Leninism is ambivalent in its understanding of language, as it is in most matters. On the one hand, everyone who knows this theory has learnt that the dominant language is always the language of the dominant classes. On the other hand, they have learnt too that an idea that has gripped the masses becomes a material force, and that on this basis Marxism itself is (or will be) victorious because it is correct. In what follows, it will be shown that the structure of communist society depends precisely on this ambivalence. But first another question needs to be explored: how ought this 'ideal' linguistic compulsion function – this compulsion that can 'seize' individual people and potentially also the masses – if it is to transform thereby into a revolutionary force of constitutive power?

Chapter One

The Linguistification of Society

Plato was the first in the Western philosophical tradition to elevate language to the medium of total power and the total transformation of society. In *The Republic* he declares the rule of the philosophers to be the telos of social development. Plato defines the philosopher, in contrast to the sophist, as someone who does not use language to represent, legitimate and defend private and partial interests, but instead conceives of society as a whole. But to think the totality of society means to think the totality of the language that this society speaks. This is what differentiates philosophy from science or art, each of which uses specialized language of one form or another. Science claims to employ only language that is free of contradiction and logically valid. Art claims to employ language in an aesthetically challenging way. Philosophy, by contrast, uses language in such a way that it addresses the whole of language. But to think and address the whole of language necessarily implies laying claim to the government of the society that speaks this language. In this sense communism stands in the Platonic tradition: it is a modern form of Platonism in practice. On this basis, it makes sense to look to Plato for an initial answer to the question of how language can exercise sufficient force to allow the speaker to rule over and through language.

For Socrates, hero of the Platonic dialogues, the force of conviction radiated by the smooth and well-constructed speeches of the sophists in no way suffices for government. Only the force of logic would be sufficient for that, for the only aspect of a speech that has an effect which cannot be evaded by those confronted with it is its logical evidence. The listener or reader of an evident statement can of course wilfully decide to contradict the compelling effect of this statement, asserting by this resistance an inner, absolute, subjective freedom with regard to all external constraints, including those of logic. But someone who adopts such a counter-evident position does not even really believe it himself, as is often said in such cases. Those who do not accept what is logically evident as such become internally divided, and this division weakens them in comparison to those who accept and affirm the evidence. The acceptance of logical evidence makes one stronger; to reject it, conversely, is to grow weaker. For classical philosophy, the power of reason becomes manifest here: reason is the power capable of internally weakening and even ultimately vanquishing the enemies of reason – those who reject what is evident – solely through language and logic, solely by exercising the force of logic.

But this raises the question of how such logical evidence can and should be generated. An initial assumption might be that what is logically evident appears in an act of speech that contains no internal contradictions and, being thus coherent, presents a consistent argument. Mathematics is usually held up as a model for this kind of evidence. And indeed, anyone who is confronted with the statement a + b = b + a can hardly defy the evidence of this statement. But how is such logical evidence made available within political arguments, which do not invoke the axioms and theorems of mathematics, but instead try to formulate what is good and what is harmful for the state? For Plato, at least at first glance, the criterion of logically valid, convincing speech likewise appears to be its coherence, that is to say, its lack of internal contradiction. Whenever Socrates diagnoses an internal contradiction in a speaker, he immediately disqualifies that speech as non-evident, exposing the speaker as unfit for the just exercise of state power. Socrates' questions break through the smooth, glittering surfaces of sophistical speech and uncover its contradictory, paradoxical core. It emerges that such speech only superficially appears to be well-knit and coherent. In its internal logical structure, however, it is obscure and dark because it is paradoxical. Hence such speech cannot serve as a manifestation of clear and evident thinking, but is good only as a commodity in the marketplace of ideas. The principal reproach directed by Socrates against the sophists is that they compose their speeches solely for the sake of payment. This allows an initial definition to be given for the functioning of paradox: a paradox that conceals its paradoxical nature becomes a commodity.

But how does one achieve a language so completely evident that it no longer merely circulates as a dark and obscure commodity in the marketplace of ideas, but instead becomes capable of serving the transparent self-reflection of thought? For only a language whose evidence is internal, and not merely superficial, can generate the persuasive force capable of governing the world. At first glance, it indeed appears plausible that completely evident speech should be contradiction-free, coherent and logically valid. Systematic efforts to generate such paradox-free speech begin at the latest with Aristotle and continue to the present day. But observant readers of the Platonic dialogues will have noticed that Socrates, for his part, in no way endeavours to produce coherent and paradox-free speech. He is content with discovering and revealing the paradoxes in the speeches of his opponents. And rightly so, for simply by exposing the paradoxes hidden beneath the surface of sophistical speech, evidence of such intense effulgence shines forth that listeners and readers of the Platonic dialogues become fascinated, and for lengthy periods are unable to tear themselves away from him. It is entirely sufficient to point out the hidden paradox, to uncover it, to disclose it, for the required evidence to arise.

The further step of formulating a contradiction-free discourse is unnecessary. The reader already trusts Socrates' words thanks to this evidence radiating solely from the paradoxes that Socrates has exposed. In light of this evidence, Socrates acquires the right to talk in myths, examples and suggestive analogies – and nonetheless achieves credibility. Nor does Socrates ever contend that genuinely paradox-free speech is actually possible, or even desirable – speech, in other words, of perfect sophistry, which would be coherent not only superficially but also internally. To the contrary, Socrates not only uncovers the paradoxes of others, he also makes paradox the basis for his own activity simply by positioning himself as a 'philosopher', that is, as someone who, while certainly loving and seeking wisdom in the sense of perfectly contradiction-free and self-evident speech, neither possesses such wisdom now nor in all probability ever will. There can never be a perfect sophist. The ideal of entirely contradiction-free speech remains forever unattainable – and is fundamentally superfluous.

Socrates only appears to pursue the discovery of the paradoxes that he diagnoses in sophistical speech with critical intent, that is, with the aim of cleansing this speech of its paradoxicality. What Socrates actually shows is that no speech can avoid being contradictory. If we understand philosophical thinking to be the exposure of the inner logical structure of a discourse, then from the perspective of genuine thinking, the logical composition of any discourse can be described in no other way than as self-contradiction, as paradox. *Logos* is paradox. The impression of an absence of contradiction can be conveyed only by the rhetorical surfaces of speech. The democratic demand for the equal rights of all opinions and discourses correlates with this Socratic insight into the paradoxical composition of every discourse, of every speech and of every opinion. Under the conditions of democratic freedom of opinion, opinions cannot actually be classified into 'coherent' or 'true' opinions and 'incoherent' or 'untrue' opinions. Such a division would be blatantly discriminatory and anti-democratic. It would be anti-democratic because it would undermine the equal opportunities of opinions and encroach upon their free and fair competition in the open marketplace of ideas. The axiom of the democratic marketplace of ideas states that there is no privileged metaphysical, metalinguistic position that would allow distinctions to be drawn between opinions not only with respect to their success in the marketplace of ideas but also with respect to their truth, be that the truth of logical coherence or empirical truth. In the context of the free circulation of opinions, it can be stated only that some opinions are more popular or more able to win over a majority than others, without them automatically becoming 'more true' as a result. Although there is a widespread prejudice to the contrary, Nietzsche is in fact one of the most rigorous thinkers of democracy and at the same time the prophet of the free market, for he abolished the privileges of 'true speech' and proclaimed the equal rights of all opinions. It would be futile and moreover very nearly reactionary to attempt to re-institute a distinction today between true and untrue ideas. What needs to be established instead is that every *doxa* is paradoxical. As had already been shown by Socrates, no one who speaks under the conditions of freedom of opinion knows what he actually means. Although most people believe that their ideas contradict other ideas, and are polemically directed against other ideas, these ideas in fact contradict only themselves. Every speaker says what he intends to mean, but he also says the opposite of this. All the opinions that circulate in the free market of ideas are characterized equally by this state of internal contradiction, internal paradox. For this reason, the philosopher can conceive of what is common to all discourses, of the totality of discourse, and can transcend mere opinion in this way without thereby asserting a claim to the truth of his own opinion. Indeed, the philosopher actually has no meaning of his own at all – he is simply not a sophist. Philosophical thought is established not at the level of individual opinion, but rather at the transindividual level of what is logically common to all discourses. This more profound logical level, which transcends the surfaces of the free marketplace of opinions, is the level of the self-contradiction, the paradox that forms the internal logical structure of all opinions. The difference between sophistical discourse and philosophical discourse consists solely in that philosophy explicitly thematizes the self-contradiction that sophistical discourse seeks to hide. Therefore when Plato asserts in *The Republic* that the philosophers should rule the state, and takes the philosophers to be those who by definition are not wise but merely strive for wisdom, a paradox is invoked that is clearly intended by Socrates to be the greatest possible paradox, one capable of grasping the paradoxical composition of any discourse whatsoever. This paradox, by which Socrates describes his own situation, should not be eliminated or transcended, nor should it be deconstructed. Instead, this paradox provides the basis for the philosopher's political claim to power. Thus it becomes clear that, for Plato, only paradox is capable of generating the evidence required for governing the world by the force of logic. The Platonic state is founded on the evidence of a paradox and is administered by that paradox. The principal flaw of sophistical speech consists solely in the fact that it hides its paradoxical condition, not in the fact that it is paradoxical. Instead of letting the paradox shine forth, the sophist obscures it by hiding it behind the smooth surfaces of a discourse that only appears to be coherent and logically valid. Paradox then ceases to be the place where the logical structure of language is revealed most clearly, and instead becomes the dark core of a glittering speech that is inevitably suspected by listeners of harbouring the hidden influence of private interests, secret manipulations and unconfessed desires. For as is generally known, interests and desires are obscure and ambivalent. It could be said that sophistical speech replaces the logical evidence of paradox with the obscure ambivalence of the feelings. The work of the philosopher, by contrast, consists in allowing the purely logical and linguistic composition of the paradox to shine forth – and thereby simultaneously bringing to light and transforming into light the dark core of speech that is only apparently logically valid.

The sophist is an entrepreneur who offers the empty surfaces of coherently articulated speech to anyone who wishes to be concealed behind them. The real attraction of the linguistic commodities offered for sale by the sophist is represented less by their logically valid surfaces than by the dark space behind those surfaces, where customers can settle in comfortably. Listeners are encouraged to appropriate the obscure core of sophistical speech in order to fill it with their own concerns. In other words, speech that hides its paradoxical structure becomes a commodity that invites penetration into its paradoxical interior. But all speech that is presented as logically valid is sophistical. The dark space of the paradox, which lies concealed beneath the surface of coherently constructed speech, can never be entirely eliminated. It is true that the rules of formal logic seek to exclude paradox completely. But we know, at least since Russell and Gödel, that even mathematics is paradoxical, particularly when mathematical propositions refer to themselves and to the whole of mathematics. The self-referentiality of language, however, is impossible to escape. Of course, an outright prohibition can be placed on speaking about the whole of language and about the *logos* as such, as Wittgenstein once demanded. However, such a prohibition is not only unnecessarily repressive, but is also once again contradictory in itself, for one must speak about the whole of language to be able to prohibit such speech. Ultimately, every proposition can be interpreted as a proposition about the whole of language because every proposition belongs to the whole of language.

Sophistical speech appears to be coherent only because it is one-sided, because it is cut off from the whole, and because it obscures its paradoxical relationship to the whole of language. The sophist continues to deliver his plea for a particular position even though he knows that there is much to be said at the same time for the opposing position. In endeavouring to lend his utterance coherence and consistency, the sophist employs in his speech only those arguments that strengthen the position he represents, passing over all possible opposing arguments in silence. The sophist thereby replaces the whole of language with the whole of capital.

The most important rule of formal logic, which all coherently constructed speech professes to follow, is *tertium non datur*. This *tertium*, however, which is excluded from coherently organized language, becomes money – and, as the obscure core of language, begins to rule over it both externally and internally, transforming it into a commodity. The conflict of positions, each of which represents a distinct, private, one-sided and particular interest in a coherent and consistent manner, leads ultimately to compromise. Compromise is indispensible in such arguments because it alone can bring peace between the conflicting parties, and thus preserve the unity of the whole society. Compromise simultaneously accepts and endorses two opposing assertions, A and not-A, and in consequence its form is actually that of a paradox. But in contrast to the paradox, compromise is formulated in the medium of money, not in the medium of language. In other words, compromise involves financially compensating both the advocates of A and the advocates of not-A for accepting the truth of the opposing position. The sophists, who have argued in favour of both sides, receive financial compensation in just this way. It could be said, therefore, that when paradox is replaced by compromise, power over the whole passes from language to money. A compromise is a paradox that is paid not to reveal itself to be a paradox.

The philosopher, by contrast, allows the full logical evidence of the hidden paradox to shine forth. This brilliant radiance of the paradox is due first to the effect of sudden sincerity, the unconcealing of what had been concealed, the exposure of what had previously remained beneath the surface. Sophistical speech is internally structured by paradox, and as long as this paradox remains obscure, sophistical speech is necessarily suspected of being manipulative and of serving obscure interests. The philosopher confirms this suspicion by exposing the paradoxical core of sophistical speech. As a result, this suspicion is converted into unconditional trust in the philosopher who has performed the exposure, albeit only for a certain time. The addressee of sophistical speech is the people. But the people are fundamentally mistrustful. In particular, they mistrust slick, well-constructed, eloquent speech. The speaker may be admired on account of his eloquence, but he is not trusted. Socrates makes the people's mistrust his own, and agitates against the sophists in the name of this popular mistrust. It is no coincidence that people who work with their hands, such as shipwrights or physicians, are always mentioned with praise in Socrates' speeches, and held up as positive models in opposition to the lying sophists. And yet, at the same time, Socrates asserts the supremacy of those who concern themselves with the whole, with the totality, rather than pursuing only partial occupations, as the majority of the people do. Socrates' strategy is also paradoxical in tactical respects: he allies himself with the people against the educated elite, and simultaneously with the elite against the people. Everyone is equally irritated by this, to be sure. But that scarcely troubles the philosopher, for the philosopher wants to lead, not to mislead. And for that he requires not darkness but light. The philosopher wants to be a ruler who fascinates, illuminates, dazzles and leads with the light of the revealed paradox.

Yet this complicated play of trust and mistrust, which continually produces the effect of evidence, is insufficient in itself to explain the specific composition of the evidence that appears when a paradox is revealed by philosophical discourse. This evidence has a quite particular character because it bears reference to totality. A paradox is an icon of the whole of language. That is, a paradox consists in simultaneously holding A and not-A in the mind as true. But the whole of language is nothing other than thinking the unity of all possible propositions A and not-A – which follows already from the fact that, according to the rules of formal logic, all the sentences of language can be derived from paradox. A paradox is an icon of language because it offers a viewpoint over the totality of language. But a paradox is only the icon of language, and not for instance its mimetic image, because the paradox does not reflect an always existing and pre-given linguistic totality. Rather, the paradox is what first allows this totality to take shape. As a representation of God, an icon in the Christian tradition is similarly an image for which there is no original, for the God of Christianity is invisible. The paradox that is discovered – or rather created – by the philosopher is an icon of the *logos* as a whole, and precisely for this reason the evidence it possesses and radiates is absolute, for this evidence cannot be obscured by any comparison to an original. The light of the evidence produced by exposing a paradox can be exhausted over time, however. As the Russian Formalists might say, with time a paradox is 'automatized' and is no longer perceived as a paradox but is instead perceived almost as something that can be taken for granted. Then the paradox grows obscure, just as old icons darken with age. When this happens, the paradox in question must either be restored, or replaced by a new paradox, by a new icon of the *logos*. Of course, not all paradoxes become iconic paradoxes – those that give off such an intense effulgence of evidence, and represent the whole of the *logos* so brightly, that they generate a surplus of evidence sufficient to allow the whole field of politics to be governed philosophically, at least for a certain historical period.

Throughout its entire history, philosophy has constantly tried to discover or invent new paradoxes in order to gain the upper hand over one-sided scientific and political discourse. The history of philosophy can be represented as a collection of iconic paradoxes, in which each radiates its own evidence without contradicting the others, for paradoxes cannot contradict each other. That is why the so-called theories of philosophy can coexist peacefully – so-called because they are not in fact theories at all – whereas scientific theories are in competition with one another. The will to paradox already played a decisive role when Descartes provided Western philosophy with a new foundation: thinking subjectivity was understood by Descartes to be the location and medium of doubt. With regard to the self-contradictory opinions with which the listening or reading philosopher is constantly confronted, the Cartesian *epoché* means nothing other than the decision to live in paradox, to endure paradox, for the decision to suspend all opinions is logically just as paradoxical as the decision to affirm or to reject all opinions. The effulgence of evidence emanating from this paradox has illuminated all modernity. And this paradox alone makes Descartes' apparently coherent and methodologically correct expositions plausible – for on closer examination, the formal-logical evidence being presented is quite problematic. The evidence of the Cartesian method is borrowed evidence, borrowed from the paradox that this method takes as its point of departure. When the Cartesian *epoché* is later repeated by Husserl in another form, Husserl's ostensibly evident phenomenological method likewise lives de facto upon the evidence of the paradox represented by the phenomenological *epoché*.

The search for newly brilliant paradoxes has intensified even further in recent decades, above all in French philosophy. Whatever else needs to be said about the individual discourses of Bataille, Foucault, Lacan, Deleuze or Derrida, one thing cannot be disputed: they all speak in paradoxes; they affirm paradox; they strive for an ever more radical and all-embracing paradox; they oppose all efforts to flatten out paradox and to subsume it within formal-logically valid discourse. In this way, these authors actually locate themselves in the best philosophical tradition, namely the Platonic tradition. But at the same time, they see themselves – and each, to be sure, in his own way – as dissidents from this tradition. For these authors, that is, paradox does not radiate the evidence of reason, but instead reveals the obscure Other of reason, of the subject, of *logos*. Paradox arises for these authors as a consequence of language being occupied from the outset by the forces of desire, of the corporeal, of the festival, of the unconscious, of the sacred, of the traumatic – and/or as a consequence of the materiality, the corporeality of language itself; that is to say, paradox arises at the linguistic, rhetorical surfaces of discourse, and not at the more profound hidden levels of its logical structure. Consequently, the shattering of the surfaces of an apparently coherent and 'rational' discourse is not interpreted as the revelation of the internal logical structure of this discourse – that structure which is necessarily paradoxical – but is interpreted instead as a manifestation of the Other of *logos*, which acts directly upon the surfaces of language and, by flowing through these surfaces, infiltrates and deconstructs all the logical oppositions that allow a coherent discourse to be fashioned. This peculiar gesture of the self-abnegation of philosophical thought can only be understood if it is borne in mind that these authors clearly accept only formal-logically valid, coherent and contradiction-free language to be the language of reason. Everything that is paradoxical is exiled from reason and situated in the Other of reason. Only the subject of coherent language – that is, only the sophist – is here regarded as the subject of reason. But because it is claimed at the same time that a genuinely coherent language is impossible, the subject of reason is declared to be dead – or at a minimum, is banished to the obscure kingdom of shadows that lies beyond reason. This revolt against the subject of sophistical, formal-logically valid discourse is additionally understood to be a political revolt against the institutions of the dominant power, for capitalist modernity is diagnosed as a territory ruled by the reason of clear, calculating and contradiction-free argument. Readers of Foucault indeed receive the impression that modern industry, prisons, hospitals and the police have only a single goal: to force humans to submit to the authority of formal-logically valid reason. And for many, this authority appears to be total, and every revolt against it seems doomed to failure. Power and knowledge, both structured according to the rules of formal logic, here constitute a unity from which no speaker can escape, because there is no speaker who can avoid arguing coherently. On this basis the encounter with the Other of reason also proves to be an impossible task for Derrida, for it is impossible to see darkness in the dark. Only against all reason can deconstruction hope for such an encounter; it can never achieve it. The 'system' is too strong. Reason is too almighty. Rational calculation is too unavoidable. To be sure, the revolt against reason is necessary, but it is also impossible, because the rule of reason cannot be broken. That is why those who speak in paradoxes today appear as *philosophes maudits* who – traumatized by life, driven by the forces of desire, and hopelessly gone astray in the obscurity of language – explode or deconstruct rational discourse with paradox.

In this diagnosis, modernity is governed by reason that operates and calculates formal-logically and that places us helplessly at the mercy of its power. But to an unprejudiced observer, this diagnosis appears as nothing less than astonishing; here the real relations of power are truly turned on their heads. In reality, sophistical and apparently rational discourses still serve the market and particular interests today as they have always done. Rationality here is in no sense the insignia of power, but instead functions as the 'design' of a linguistic commodity that conforms to the market. There is no such thing as the total rule of reason, of the system, or of structure. It is common knowledge that the hand which governs the market is invisible; that is, that it operates in the dark, in paradox. The whole of capitalism appears in the medium of money, not in the medium of language, and most particularly not in the medium of a rational language. As is generally known, success in the market does not depend on calculation, on coolly logical reasoning or rational reflection; instead, it requires intuition, obsessiveness, aggressiveness and killer instinct. Therefore, discourse that seeks out reason's obscure Other is in no way oppositional with respect to capitalism. The discourse of desire appears to be iconoclastic because it smashes the smooth surfaces of coherent speech so that these surfaces can no longer serve as a medium for the representation of certain matters of fact, for the formulation of certain projects, for arguing in favour of certain points of view, or for presenting certain 'visions'. And the institutions that use and administer such speech are also implicated in such a critique. But these institutions are not institutions of power. For its part, capitalism in fact lives by criticizing institutions and subverting stable worldviews. It translates convictions into interests and makes compromises that have the structure of paradoxes. Only sophistical, instrumental language is affected by criticism directed against the ideal of self-transparent rationality.

The discovery of the paradoxical core of a sophistical speech awakens a suspicion that is much more profound than the belief that behind reason, reason's Other lies concealed. What is instead awoken is the suspicion that behind the surfaces of conventional and lucid reason another reason is hiding, diabolical, evil and obscure – a reason that thinks in paradoxes and that profits equally from all opposing positions. The sophists were always seen as such unconfessed diabolists, capable of arguing equally convincingly for diametrically opposed positions. But it is capital that should be pre-eminently regarded as diabolical, because capital can profit from A as well as from not-A. If the workers receive higher wages, they can buy more – and profits grow. If the workers receive lower wages, savings can be made on labour power – and profits continue to grow. If there is peace, profits grow thanks to stability. If there is war, profits grow on account of the new demand, and so on. The impression thus arises that capital is by no means anonymous, but rather that behind capital a diabolical subject is hiding, a subject that plays a 'win-win' game that it alone always wins because it profits equally from opposing outcomes. However, this more profound suspicion can be neither confirmed nor disproved, for this diabolical subject can be represented only in black on black, and thus cannot be seen. But precisely for this reason the diabolical subject is suspected of governing the world as a whole, in its totality, because the world appears to us as a unity of opposites, as an ontological paradox that can never be perfectly resolved into coherent discourse.

Now the philosophical subject – in other words, the revolutionary subject – is constituted precisely by appropriating this diabolical reason, which otherwise remains hidden and operates in darkness, and transforming it into dialectical reason by means of its linguistification. Only the suspicion that there is not just capital, but also a world conspiracy of capital – that is to say, a power that operates behind and by means of capital and that always triumphs whenever capital wins, which is to say, literally always – only such a suspicion leads to the constitution of the subject who wishes to reveal and appropriate this power. It could easily be said that such a suspicion is paranoid, unfounded, unprovable and ultimately a slanderous lie. However, every revolution begins with a lie, as Alexandre Kojève justly remarks in his commentaries on Hegel's *Philosophy of Right*. With equal justification, Kojève also points out that the responsibility for the emergence of such a slander does not rest with those who formulate and utter the slander, but with the rulers, who, by virtue of the obscure and opaque aura of power that surrounds them, first create the possibility of allowing this suspicion to emerge.[1]

1 Alexandre Kojève, *Introduction à la lecture de Hegel*, Paris: Gallimard, 1947, 136ff.

Revolutionary suspicion is the effect of paranoia. But this is not a case of 'subjective' paranoia, which could be cured psychiatrically or psychoanalytically, but rather of an 'objective' paranoia, the conditions of whose emergence lie in the object itself, which arouses suspicion by appearing as an obscure object, one that recoils from the coherent arguments of reason. The whole world appears to us in this way as just such an obscure object, one that necessarily arouses the suspicion of harbouring in its interior a diabolical reason that rules through paradoxes. In the Western cultural context, capital rarely falls under such suspicion. But the example of terrorism provides a good illustration of the operation of this suspicion, for in recent years terrorism has become an object of objective paranoia.

Today, for instance, when Western politicians call for a war on terrorism and simultaneously for the preservation of traditional civil rights, there is a paradox, for these aims contradict each other. In this case the usual tendency is to speak of a politics that makes compromises between two demands – the demands for security and for civic freedoms. But the word 'compromise' is misleading here. One could speak of compromise if in society there were two groups of the population, one of which wanted the preservation of freedoms, including freedom for terrorism, and the other which wanted the abolition of all freedoms, including the freedom of terrorism. But it is perfectly clear that two such groups do not exist – or, if they do exist, then both groups are too marginal. It simply does not pay to fashion a compromise between such marginal groups. Those who believe in these two logically valid alternatives are instead categorized as freaks – as freedom freaks or as security freaks – and accordingly are not taken seriously. The 'healthy' majority of the population, just like the reigning policy, does not believe in these contradiction-free alternatives, but rather believes in paradox, and calls for a dialectical politics of paradox. This demand follows from the suspicion that the politics of terror is a diabolical politics – which thus requires a dialectical, paradoxical response. In other words, the initial assumption is that the terrorists want to abolish the 'liberal social order'. In that case, the terrorists will win equally if either of the two contradiction-free alternatives is realized consistently: either terror is successful because it is granted free rein for its terrorist activities, or it is successful because civic freedoms are abolished in the anti-terrorist struggle.

The question of whether terrorist reason is actually diabolical is irrelevant. It suffices to say that 'the motives of the terrorists are obscure' to license the suspicion that such a diabolical reason lurks behind the deeds of the terrorists. Here it is important to note only that when such an obscure object of objective paranoia arises, the response to it necessarily becomes dialectical and paradoxical. The genuine political discourse of modernity therefore appears to be fundamentally different from the way it is usually represented. In most accounts, that is, only those who think coherently and formal-logically are regarded as normal within the context of rationalist modernity. Conversely, those who think paradoxically are marginalized or declared to be crazy, abnormal or at best to be *poètes maudits*. But reality seems to be precisely the reverse of this. In our time, only those who think and live in permanent self-contradiction count as normal, as mainstream. The famous 'centrist politics' is really a politics of paradox that only barely manages to conceal its paradoxical character behind an illusion of compromise. Today, those who seek to argue in formal-logically valid, coherent and conclusive ways are by contrast regarded as marginal, if not simply as crazy, and in any case as 'unworldly' and unfit for the exercise of power.

Now, Soviet power explicitly defined itself as the rule of dialectical, paradoxical reason – as the answer to the paradoxical character of capital and the commodity as described by Marx. The Communist Party combats the conspiracy of capital by appropriating this conspiracy, forming a counter-conspiracy and moving itself, as the subject of this counter-conspiracy, into the centre of society – namely, as the governing party. Communist revolution involves exposing, confirming and materializing the suspicion that behind the illusion of an open society are hidden the closed spaces of a manipulative and conspiratorial power located in obscure paradox. The exposure, proclamation and appropriation of this paradox are genuine philosophical achievements, which empower the philosophers to rule. Soviet power must be interpreted primarily as an attempt to realize the dream of all philosophy since its Platonic foundation, that of the establishment of the kingdom of philosophy. Every communist leader who held himself to be anything at all understood himself as a philosopher, as one whose praxis represented in the first place a contribution to the development of communist theory. In this regard a practical defeat could be understood as just as instructive, and thus as valuable, as a success. In this, incidentally, communist power can be distinguished from the fascist regimes with which it is often compared. These regimes, though also totalitarian, are namely not total enough. Fascist discourse remains sophistical because it explicitly professes to prosecute the claims of a certain race or a certain state against other races or states. By contrast, communist, dialectical-materialist discourse alone takes the whole to be its object. This certainly does not mean that this discourse recognizes no enemies; it does mean, however, that this discourse does not renounce its sovereign power of determining for itself who its enemies are. Communism recognizes no friend–enemy relation that precedes and determines it. Even when the communist movement professes to defend the interests of the working class against the class of the bourgeoisie, the division of society into distinct classes that lies at the basis of this claim is for its part a product of Marxist theory. The communist leadership accordingly always reserved for itself the right of determining who should be declared to belong to the proletariat and who to the bourgeoisie, and when and why they so belonged. To be total means to have no enemies – outside of those whom one has knowingly and deliberately made for oneself.

Chapter Two

When Paradox Holds Power

The Soviet Union understood itself literally as a state governed by philosophy alone. Specifically, the communist leadership was principally legitimated as a leadership because it represented a certain philosophical theory, Marxism–Leninism. The leadership had no other legitimation. Hence the pre-eminent duty of the communist leadership was always that of philosophizing. Marxist–Leninist theory was understood here as the unity of dialectical materialism, historical materialism and scientific communism. Dialectical materialism was regarded as the most important and decisive part of this triad, for the other parts could be derived by applying the general theory of dialectical materialism to the understanding of history and to the planning of the communist future.

The central law of dialectical materialism is that of the unity and the conflict of opposites. To follow this law means, de facto, to think in paradoxes, and thus to seek out the greatest possible and most radical paradox as the goal of thought. Without question, this search for an ever greater paradox as the logical and linguistic icon of the whole was inherited by dialectical materialism from the Hegelian dialectic. But Hegel uses the effulgence of evidence that is radiated by his paradoxical discourse solely in order to legitimate the modern state, which he views as no longer paradoxical. Paradoxical thinking, according to Hegel, belongs to the past. Here Hegel basically repeats a figure of thought that has already been encountered in Plato and Descartes: an ultimate paradox is formulated (the wisest is the one who has no wisdom; or, only he who doubts everything, including his own existence, knows that he exists) and the evidence of this paradox is then used to legitimate a subsequent discourse that is no longer paradoxical but is instead formal-logically valid. In opposition to this Hegelian banishment of paradox into the past, Kierkegaard objected that the paradox of belief, consisting in the belief that the divine is to be found only in a certain individual finitude and not in every finitude (for example, only in Jesus Christ, not in any wandering preacher or whoever), cannot be banished into the past.[2] The paradox should not merely provide the basis for ruling; it should also exercise rule.

Dialectical materialism, however, is nothing other than the assertion that contradictions cannot be localized solely in the past, for 'material reality' as such is internally contradictory

2 Søren Kierkegaard, *Philosophical Fragments*, trans. Howard V. Hong and Edna H. Hong, Princeton: Princeton University Press, 1985, 65ff.

and paradoxical. Even when contradictions have been discovered and reflected 'in spirit', they cannot be eliminated, but continue to remain active in reality. Contradictions cannot be sublated or confined to the memory. They can only be administered, and this administration must be real and material. The 'material' of dialectical materialism does not mean the primacy of matter as it is understood in positivist science. The key formulation of dialectical materialism, as all Soviet students had to learn, states that being determines consciousness. The word 'matter' does not appear in this formula at all. And by 'being', nothing is understood here other than the (self-)contradictoriness of the world in its totality, which determines individual consciousness because consciousness cannot avoid becoming involved in these contradictions.

To think dialectical-materialistically therefore means to think consistently in terms of contradiction and paradox. All the central formulations of dialectical materialism are distinguished by their rigorous paradoxicality. And conversely, every attempt to reduce the degree of the paradoxicality of dialectical materialism – to flatten out or even to eliminate this paradoxicality – was condemned as a symptom of 'one-sidedness', of an inability to think the contradictions inherent to the whole. The reproach of one-sidedness played the same role in the logical regime of dialectical materialism as the reproach of internal contradictoriness in the context of formal logic. If a proposition was categorized as one-sided and undialectical, it was automatically rejected and its author disqualified. But to be one-sided meant roughly the same as to be formal-logically valid, to be non-paradoxical. The logical regime of dialectical materialism was diametrically opposed to the logical regime of bourgeois, formal-logical thought. Statements that were paradoxical and consequently invalid from the perspective of formal logic were, from the perspective of dialectical materialism, the only truths that could grasp reality. It was logical and contradiction-free propositions that were conversely rejected as being one-sided and consequently invalid.

The demand for a maximum of internal contradiction applied not only to philosophy, but also to political discourse. An early example is the famous debate that erupted with great intensity in the left wing of Russian social democracy in 1908. The question under discussion was whether the left should participate in the elections that were held under the supervision and according to the rules of the Tsarist regime, and send representatives to the Duma (parliament); or whether the Tsarist regime should no longer be recognized as legitimate, and the struggle against the regime should instead move underground. The Party was deeply divided by this question into 'Liquidators', who wanted to renounce the underground struggle and reorganize social democracy as a party that operated entirely legally, and the 'Otzovists', who demanded that the social democratic representatives leave the Duma and that the entire Party move underground. It was at this point that Lenin suggested a solution for this problem that became an accepted standard: representatives should be sent to the Duma, and the regime, including the Duma, should also be combated underground. For Lenin, the paradox, consisting in the fact that in this case the Party would be fighting against the representatives that it itself had sent to the Duma, did not constitute any reason to question his proposal. Entirely to the contrary: for Lenin, it was precisely the paradoxicality of his proposal that made it dialectical and consequently correct – correct insofar as the proletarian struggle made reference in this way to the whole social field. The struggle was conducted both within the Duma through peaceful means, and also outside the Duma by preparing for revolution. The advantage of formulating a political programme as a paradox here becomes clear: the totality of the political field is brought into view, and one is able to act not through exclusion but through inclusion.

Subsequent Party debates proceeded in the same way. Each debate concluded with a formulation that had the form of a paradox. Thus, after the revolution, Trotsky argued for organizing the workers in a quasi-military manner, disciplined and ready for action, and for compelling the peasants to feed and maintain these proletarian labour armies. Others, such as Bukharin and Rykov, were more moderate. They wanted to allow the peasants to 'grow into' socialism in the most peaceful way possible, and were prepared to accept that industry might develop somewhat more slowly as a result. These constituted the left and right deviations from the general line of the Party. The struggle between these positions determined the life of the country for a considerable period until the general line, represented by Stalin, won out at the beginning of the 1930s, whereupon left and right deviationists were liquidated over the course of the decade. But how was this general line defined? It can be formulated as the sum of the demands of the left and right oppositions. In all Stalin's texts and speeches, just as in the official Party documents of the time, there is nothing to be found that cannot already be recognized from the speeches and writings of the various oppositions. The only difference – but one that is all-important – consists in the fact that here the conflicting demands of the different oppositions within the Party were simultaneously accepted and asserted. Thus, for example, the most rapid possible development of industry would have to be combined with the flourishing of agriculture, and these would reciprocally and dialectically condition each other, et cetera.

The logic of internal Party debates of this period can therefore be summarized as follows: it was not what was asserted that led to a deviation being designated as such; the basis for this was instead the refusal to accept that the opposite of what had been asserted was an equally true assertion. It was on these grounds that the deviationists were disqualified as 'one-sided'. And indeed, all their demands were accepted by the general line; all their claims were always already accommodated and taken into account by the ruling paradox. The question might be asked, therefore: what did the deviationists actually still want? The answer could only be that they wanted not just something but everything, in that they not only asserted something – and this was recognized as thoroughly legitimate – but they also went further, denying and negating the opposite of what it was they had asserted. For formal logic, which strives to render its propositions free from contradiction, this second step – the negation of the opposite of what has been asserted – does not actually represent a genuine further step at all. The negation of the opposite of what has been asserted appears to be a merely trivial consequence of the first assertion itself. But for dialectical materialism, this second step is logically independent of the first step, and moreover it is this second step that is critical, for it is precisely this step that determines the difference between life and death.

Dialectical materialism believes that life is internally contradictory. For this reason, dialectical materialism seeks to grasp life through paradoxes so as to be able to govern over it. In other words, for dialectical materialism only the whole, the totality, is living. If it says A, therefore, then it does not simultaneously wish to forbid saying not-A, for if not-A were forbidden, it would mean that not-A has been excluded from the whole, and the whole would then cease to be whole and living. In addition, dialectical materialism seeks not only to speak about life; it wishes moreover that this discourse itself become living. And for dialectical materialism, to be living means simply to be contradictory and paradoxical. Machines are indeed principally distinguished from humans in that they think formal-logically validly. If a machine is confronted with a paradox, it must break down. Humans, conversely, are able to live and thrive amidst and through paradox. And furthermore, humans can in fact truly live only within the paradox that discloses the totality of life to them. A sharp distinction between totality and universality needs to be marked here. The universality of a proposition means its general validity. But from the perspective of dialectical materialism, a proposition's claim to general validity appears simply as radical one-sidedness, because the alternative has thus been entirely excluded. Those who claim for their one-sided and logically valid propositions the status of universality thus act contrary to the dialectical reason of the Party, which does not think universally, but totally.

Once this had been established, the fate of the various oppositions was sealed. They were all accused by the Stalinist leadership of wanting to kill communist language, which was living because it was paradoxical, with their one-sided, universalist, formal-logically valid and ostensibly contradiction-free formulations. Only those who were prepared to speak in a living way remained true to the general line, and thus remained alive – that is to say, only those who had understood that the validity of a given assertion fell far short of establishing that the opposite of this assertion was invalid. In contrast to formal logic or the dialectical logic of Hegelianism, the logic of dialectical materialism is a total logic. Formal logic excludes paradox; Hegelian dialectical logic allows paradox to fade away with time. But total logic asserts that paradox is a principle of life that takes death into account as well – that it is the icon of the whole, of the totality. Total logic is total because it allows the total as such to appear in its effulgence, because it thinks and affirms the totality of all possible propositions simultaneously. Total logic is a genuinely political logic: it is at once paradox and orthodox.

Official Soviet dialectical materialism is often seen – and with especial frequency by the Western left – as inflexible, dogmatic and thus intellectually unproductive, and ultimately as theoretically irrelevant. This characterization of official Soviet thought should be accepted, if only in a certain sense. But taken in isolation, this characterization is inadequate for a proper assessment of Soviet thought, for the meaning of the word 'dogmatic' remains unclear here. If a person is said to think dogmatically, then it is generally meant by this that the person has a certain view of the world and adheres to this view in spite of all objections that might prove that it is internally contradictory or stands in contradiction to reality. Such a lack of receptiveness is usually ascribed to personal unreasonableness, to ideologically-induced blindness, or, worse still, to a deliberate refusal to acknowledge inconvenient truths and to derive their necessary consequences. Soviet ideology is indeed distinguished by a certain immunity with regard to proofs that it is internally contradictory and also in contradiction with reality. But the basis for this immunity does not consist in its pig-headedness or unreceptiveness to these arguments. Rather, the basis for this immunity is Soviet ideology's conviction that the proof that its worldview is contradictory does not refute this worldview, but instead confirms it.

Those who studied dialectical materialism in the Soviet Union were simply astonished by Western critiques of this theory. For these critiques functioned in exactly the same way as the arguments of the various internal Soviet oppositions prior to the establishment of Stalinist orthodoxy. For some of these critiques, Stalinist orthodoxy was not humanist enough. Others found it to be too humanist, because it placed too much importance on humans and took too little account of the anonymous dynamics of social development.

For some, this orthodoxy was too dialectical. For others, it was not dialectical enough. Some found this orthodoxy to be too voluntaristic. Others in turn thought that what it lacked was precisely such activism. Innumerable further examples could be supplied. Students of dialectical materialism in the period, who found these critiques bewildering, basically received only a single piece of advice from their professors: think these critiques through in combination with each other. Whoever does that obtains dialectical materialism as the result. Thousands of publications appeared in the Soviet Union, particularly in the 1960s and '70s, criticizing Western critiques of Soviet ideology. Fundamentally, all of these publications advanced a single thesis: the critiques in question contradict one another and when taken together produce a statement of dialectical materialism. Thus the superiority of dialectical materialism over all the critiques of it was demonstrated without any great difficulty, simply by applying the rules of total logic. This application was deliberately repetitive because the situation itself was constantly recurring: Soviet ideology was criticized from two opposing positions, and thereby confirmed. This repetitiveness gave rise to the impression that dialectical materialism is an example of a closed doctrine, one that excludes all opposition. However, the opposite was in fact the case: total logic is an open logic, because it simultaneously accepts both A and not-A, and thus excludes no one.

Dialectical materialism instead functions as the exclusion of exclusion. It accepts every opposition. But what it does not accept is the refusal by this opposition to accept the opposition contrary to it. Dialectical materialism, that is, wishes to be absolutely open – and thus excludes everything that does not wish to be just as open as it is.

This type of total logic has of course a long prehistory. Without journeying too far back into the past: the dogmas of Christianity are nothing other than paradoxes. The divine trinity is described as the identity of one and three. Jesus Christ is described as the unity of the divine and the human, which are irreconcilable but also indivisible: Christ is all man, all God, and simultaneously the unity of man and God. It should already be clear from these examples that Christian orthodoxy thinks in paradoxes. At the same time, this thought is in no way illogical. Because theological thought seeks to conceive of the whole, it rigorously excludes everything that is not paradoxical enough – everything that is too formal-logically valid, coherent, contradiction-free and thus one-sided. All theological doctrines that claimed to be logically valid and, in consequence, to perceive only God in Christ, for instance, or only man, were categorized by Christian dogmatism as heresies, and their exponents were persecuted by the church. At the same time, ecclesiastical dogmatism represents nothing but the sum of these heresies. Like communist dogmatism, Christian dogmatism seeks to be totally open and inclusive – it only persecutes heresies because these heresies wish to exclude the opposing heresies.

In this way, theological thought searches for the greatest possible paradox, the one that excludes most radically the possibility of subsuming this paradox within coherent, formal-logically valid and one-sided thinking. When Tertullian states *credo quia absurdum*, he certainly does not mean that he is prepared to believe every absurdity simply because it is an absurdity. Rather, he means that only the absurdity of Christianity corresponds to the logical criteria of complete absurdity, that is, of complete paradoxicality, and on this basis Christianity alone meets the requirements of serving as the icon of the whole. The total logic of communism therefore stands within the tradition of the total logic of Christian dogmatism and its search for the complete self-contradiction. This is because communism is the most complete form of atheism – a thesis that Marx and Lenin never grew tired of reiterating. Neither formal logic nor dialectical logic allows for thinking the whole. Formal logic excludes paradox; the dialectic temporalizes paradox. 'Divine' theological thought, which can think the whole because it follows the rules of total logic, thus remains superior to any merely 'human' thought. The transition to radical atheism can be completed only through the appropriation by human reason of the total logic of paradoxical orthodoxy – and with this transition, no free and unoccupied logical space is left for the divine.

Now, it could be claimed – and indeed it was often claimed – that total logic, which argues in paradoxes, leads the people who practise it to begin at some point to think and act cynically and opportunistically. The arbitrariness of power becomes limitless, because it is no longer given any set boundaries by the rules of reason. The total logic of dialectical materialism was brilliantly parodied in this respect in Orwell's novel *1984*. However, the brilliance of this parody should not hide the fact that it represents nothing but a reflex of the effulgence of evidence originally generated by paradoxical thought itself. Total logic is still a logic. Paradoxical, dialectical reason remains reason, a reason that has its rules. It is uncommonly difficult to think consistently paradoxically. The histories of Christian and communist heresies demonstrate this difficulty in sufficient measure. Heresy is for total logic what incoherence is for formal logic. And it is at least as difficult to avoid heretical flattenings of paradox as it is to avoid paradox itself. Christian theology required centuries of intellectual effort to arrive at formulations that are completely paradoxical – or that at least appear so. It had constantly to combat heresies that weaken paradox in one direction or another, and could thus lead to theology being subjected to the rules of formal logic and losing its claim to totality. In precisely the same way, Soviet power required decades of intense and intellectually demanding debate in order to arrive at those almost perfectly paradoxical formulations brought together in Stalinist orthodoxy.

The famous *History of the Communist Party of the Soviet Union (Bolsheviks): Short Course*, written under the supervision of Stalin, recounts the history of the communist movement primarily as the history of the struggle against different heresies in the search for a perfectly paradoxical orthodoxy. Of greatest interest is the chapter dedicated exclusively to the description of dialectical and historical materialism. Legend has it that this chapter was written by Stalin himself. And indeed, to anyone who has read much by Stalin, the literary style of this chapter is unmistakably familiar. However that may be, this text is the one in which official Soviet philosophical discourse received its canonical, orthodox form from which it subsequently hardly ever deviated.

At the beginning of the chapter, dialectical materialism is characterized in the following way:

There were philosophers in ancient times who believed that the disclosure of contradictions in thought and the clash of opposite opinions was the best method of arriving at the truth. This dialectical method of thought, later extended to the phenomena of nature, developed into the dialectical method of apprehending nature, which regards the phenomena of nature as being in constant movement and undergoing constant change, and the development of nature as the result of the development of the contradictions in nature, as the result of the interaction of opposed forces in nature.[3]

Further on, Stalin (if it really is Stalin) emphasizes that the dialectical method can and should think the whole, the totality: 'The dialectical method therefore holds that no phenomenon in nature can be understood if taken by itself, isolated from surrounding phenomena.'[4] Later still, Stalin refers to the salient formulation of Lenin: ' "In its proper meaning," Lenin says, "dialectics is the study of the contradiction *within the very essence of things*." 'And Stalin then concludes: 'Such, in brief, are the principal features of the Marxist dialectical method.'[5]

It thus becomes clear that Stalin views the whole world as contradictory in itself, with these contradictions being constantly reproduced in every worldly thing. To understand the world therefore means to understand the contradiction

3   *History of the Communist Party of the Soviet Union (Bolsheviks): Short Course*, edited by a commission of the CC of the CPSU (B), Moscow: Foreign Languages Publishing House, 1939, 106.
4   Ibid., 106.
5   Ibid., 109.

that defines the configuration of the world at a given time. For Stalin, the dynamic of social development is determined above all by contradictions between base and superstructure. The forces of production are never simply expressed by the relations of production and the cultural institutions corresponding to them. The base is never merely passively reflected by the superstructure. Institutional organization and theoretical reflection can never neutrally and objectively mirror the degree of the development of the forces of production. Instead, the superstructure can either be delayed with regard to the development of the forces of production, and thus slow down social development, or it can precede this development and thus consciously impel development forwards. The first case is that of a reactionary superstructure; the second, that of a progressive superstructure.

On the one hand, Stalin asserts:

Hence, in order not to err in policy, in order not to find itself in the position of idle dreamers, the party of the proletariat must not base its activities on abstract 'principles of human reason,' but on the concrete conditions of the material life of society, as the determining force of social development; not on the good wishes of 'great men,' but on the real needs of development of the material life of society.[6]

6   Ibid., 115–6.

But on the other hand, ideas are not merely trivial:

> There are different kinds of social ideas and theories.
> There are old ideas and theories which have outlived
> their day, and which serve the interests of the moribund
> forces of society. Their significance lies in the fact that
> they hamper the development, the progress of society.
> Then there are new and advanced ideas and theories
> which serve the interests of the advanced forces of society.
> Their significance lies in the fact that they facilitate the
> development, the progress of society; and their significance
> is the greater the more accurately they reflect the needs
> of development of the material life of society . . . In this
> connection, Marx says: 'Theory becomes a material force
> as soon as it has gripped the masses.'[7]

Stalin therefore rejects those theorists who wish to grant
no active role to the superstructure in the historical process.
But he also argues equally against the other, opposed
deviation, which overemphasizes the formative role of the
superstructure:

> The fall of the utopians, including the Narodniks,
> Anarchists and Socialist-Revolutionaries, was due,

7   Ibid., 116–7.

among other things, to the fact that they did not recognize the primary role which the conditions of the material life of society play in the development of society, and, sinking to idealism, did not base their practical activities on the needs of the development of the material life of society, but, independently of and in spite of these needs, on 'ideal plans' and 'all-embracing projects' divorced from the real life of society.[8]

History is therefore described by Stalin as a process that is driven forwards by the perpetual contradiction between the base and the superstructure of society, in which neither side can ever win the upper hand.

A crucial question needs to be raised about this contradiction that drives the social process onwards, one concerning the medium in which the contradiction arises. For if base and superstructure exist in contradiction to each other and in tension with each other, then a medium must be posited that is itself neither base nor superstructure, and yet which also includes both base as well as superstructure, for it is only in such a medium that the contradiction between these two can come into being and be articulated. Stalin first addresses the question of this medium only much later, in 1950. And he answers it as follows: this medium is language.

8   Ibid., 116.

In the late writings of Stalin, appearing shortly before his death, we see a belated reflection of the revolutionary linguistic turn that had been performed politically by the Soviet Communist Party much earlier. These texts were composed by Stalin in a rather unusual form – namely as answers to questions ostensibly posed to him by 'normal' people. The first text consists of responses to the questions of an anonymous 'group of comrades of the younger generation', who are supposed to have begged Stalin to publish his ideas on linguistic questions. Following this there are answers to the questions of Comrade Krasheninnikova, who was entirely unknown and about whom no details were revealed, and later still, answers to the questions of Comrades Sanzheyev, Belkin, Furer and Kholopov, who were just as unknown to the wider readership and whose backgrounds and occupations remained mysterious. This gives rise to the impression that Stalin has here tried his hand at the literary genre of the self-conducted interview, with questions that he himself has posed being distributed amongst these fictive personae so that the text can remain fragmentary, and also to lend it a lively and provisional character. The answers were printed as a kind of serial novel in the newspaper *Pravda* over a number of days. Each new set of questions, which were attributed to a new character, were designed to render more precise and comprehensive the answers that in Stalin's opinion remained incomplete or had not yet been formulated clearly enough in the previous instalment of the dialogue. The whole undertaking is an idiosyncratic example of a public, thoroughly experimental and uncertain self-examination, which neither properly begins nor ever really ends anywhere definite. But in any case, one thing becomes clear in reading this peculiar witness to the inner life of a political leader: the reason why Stalin felt such urgency to publish these unfinished, fragmentary and provisional insights immediately was that he believed he had come upon something of great importance, and did not want to leave the world in ignorance of his discovery a moment longer.

Stalin's self-examination was originally prompted by the thesis of Soviet linguist N. Y. Marr, influential at the time, that language belonged to the superstructure. Stalin forcefully rejects this thesis, challenging the notion that language could be class-specific – as is always the case with the superstructure – and instead emphasizing that:

Language exists, and it has been created precisely in order to serve society as a whole, as a means of intercourse between people, in order to be common to the members of society and the single language of society, serving members of society equally, irrespective of their class status . . . In this respect, while it differs in principle from the superstructure, language does not differ from the implements of production, from machines, let us say, which may equally serve a capitalist system and a socialist system.[9]

It soon becomes clear why Stalin reacts so heatedly to the thesis that language has a superstructural character. The superstructure is not total. It is restricted to the extent that it differs from the base. If language belongs to the superstructure, then its operation is also restricted. But such a restriction does not please Stalin at all. And the reason for this is obvious: as everything economic in the Soviet Union was decided and controlled in language, then if language were isolated to the restricted sphere of the superstructure, then Stalin's own claim to leadership would consequently be limited, and his power to command and organize the base of Soviet society would be curtailed. It is for this reason that Stalin asserts:

> Language, on the contrary, is connected with man's productive activity directly, and not only with man's productive activity, but with all his other activities in all spheres of work, from production to the base and from the base to the superstructure . . . That is why the sphere of action of language, which embraces all spheres

9   Joseph Stalin, *Marxism and Linguistics*, New York: International Publishers, 1951, 11.

of man's activity, is far broader and more varied than the sphere of action of the superstructure. More, it is practically unlimited.[10]

But Stalin first achieves a definitive clarification of his intentions with the following formulation: 'Unlike the superstructure, which is not connected with production directly but through the economy, language is directly connected with man's productive activity, as well as with all his other activity in all his spheres of work without exception.'[11] In other words, Stalin wants to guarantee that language is awarded direct and 'immediate' access to production – that is, access that is not economically mediated – so that language becomes the medium in which the superstructure achieves the power of immediately shaping the base.

Only after the publication of his first self-conducted interview does Stalin become aware of the danger that the medium of language could be understood merely as something that connects base and superstructure, not as something that rules over them. It is this interpretation that Stalin hopes to forestall in his answer to Comrade Krasheninnikova. Once again, he stresses: 'Briefly, language cannot be ranked either among bases or among superstructures. Neither can it be

10   Ibid., 13.
11   Ibid., 24.

ranked among "intermediate" phenomena between the base and the superstructure, as such "intermediate" phenomena do not exist.' And then he asks himself, further:

> But perhaps language could be ranked among the productive forces of society, among, let us say, the implements of production? Indeed, there does exist a certain analogy between language and implements of production: Implements of production, as does language, manifest a kind of indifference towards classes and can equally serve different classes of society, both old and new. Does this circumstance provide grounds for ranking language among implements of production?[12]

But the answer is: 'No, it does not,' for language as such produces no material wealth. Language does not need to produce any, however, because it is always already material. Stalin polemicizes in this same text against Marr's idea that there can be thought without language: 'Bare thoughts, free of the language material, free of the "natural matter" of language – do not exist.'[13]

By this stage Stalin's position is sufficiently clear: language is neither superstructure nor base nor yet a productive force. But

12   Ibid., 34.
13   Ibid., 36.

equally, it is superstructure and also base and a productive force as well, because without language there is and could be nothing at all. And it is a productive force not only when it 'seizes the masses', but is rather inherently and entirely material and, circumventing the economy, is 'immediately' connected with everything material. Or to put this another way, language is capable of entirely replacing the economy, money and capital because it has direct access to all human activities and spheres of life. What is decisive for the functioning of language as such is therefore not its role as raw material in the production of various linguistic commodities that are economically connected with other spheres of life, so that the circulation of these linguistic commodities is subjected to general market conditions. Rather, language possesses the capacity to connect base and superstructure directly and immediately, thereby eliminating the market economy. Clearly, it is precisely this capacity of language that is realized in a socialist, communist society.

The definition given here to language is paradoxical and self-contradictory: language is defined as neither base nor as superstructure, nor as something that is neither base nor superstructure. But this does not disturb Stalin at all. Wholly to the contrary, he is happy to inveigh against those he terms 'textualists and Talmudists', who can be identified by their understanding of Marxism, which they treat as 'dead dogma' – and by 'dogma', Stalin here means a proposition that is internally free of contradiction, that claims to be universally valid, and that resists 'living contradiction'. Stalin reacts with corresponding severity to the reproach intended by Comrade Kholopov, who claims to have discovered a contradiction between Stalin's earlier and later assertions. Stalin does not dispute that this contradiction exists, but he refuses to accept the existence of this contradiction as something worthy of censure. He writes:

> Obviously, having discovered a contradiction between these two formulas, and believing deeply that this contradiction must be eliminated, Comrade Kholopov considers it necessary to get rid of one of the formulas as the incorrect one and to clutch at the other formula as the correct one for all times and countries, but he does not know exactly which formula to clutch at. Comrade Kholopov does not even guess that both formulas may be correct – each for its time.

And Stalin continues: 'This is always the case with textualists and Talmudists who, quoting formally without penetrating into the substance of the matter and irrespective of the historical conditions treated in the quotations, invariably land in a hopeless situation.'[14]

Stalin's affirmation of this contradiction is admittedly weakened somewhat by his reference to a sense in which the

14 Ibid., 45.

opposing formulas in question refer to different times, and hence do not really enter into contradiction with each other. Yet in this same text, Stalin emphasizes the transhistorical stability of language. And to less simple minds than that of 'Comrade Kholopov', it was quite clear that Stalin's texts on linguistics served to establish contradiction as the supreme law of logic. In the field of biology, an ideological battle was raging during this period concerning how the living could be distinguished from the dead, the mechanical, the machinic. Because genetics sought to subordinate life to a dead combinatory of signs, it was suspected by those in power of being on the side of death. The role played here by formal logic made the matter even more suspicious: formal logic was understood to be the logic of machines, not that of the human as a living being. It was with good reason that Alexander Oparin drew out the parallels between Stalin's remarks on language and the positions of Lysenko, leader of the victorious camp of the anti-geneticists, in his short book *The Significance of Stalin's Works in the Field of Linguistics for the Creative Development of Soviet Biology*.[15] In this context, Oparin cites Lysenko, for whom the aim of conception consisted in creating 'a unified, biologically contradictory body, that is, a body capable of life'. Here the

15 A.I. Oparin, *Znachenie rabot tovarishcha I.V. Stalina po voprosam iazykoznaniia dlia razvitiia sovetskoi biologicheskoi nauki*, Moscow, 1951.

formulation is entirely clear: only that which is contradictory in itself may be regarded as living, and as capable of life. The living being itself is understood as a certain logical figure – namely, the figure of paradox.

Thus Stalinist communism proves finally to be a revival of the Platonic dream of the kingdom of philosophers, those who operate by means of language alone. In the Platonic state, the language of the philosophers is converted into direct violence by the class of the guardians. This violence holds the state together. The Stalinist state was no different. It was the state apparatuses that translated the language of the philosopher into action – and, as is common knowledge, this translation was exceedingly brutal, incessantly brutal. Nevertheless, this remains a case of rule by language, for the sole means by which the philosopher could compel these apparatuses to listen to him and to act in the name of the whole were those of language. In contrast to classical monarchy, power was not legitimated by the body of the monarch – to be more precise, by the ancestral line of his body. The legitimacy of the fascist leader was similarly derived from the racial ancestry of his body, and in this sense fascism is a democratic variant of monarchy. The body of the communist leader, conversely, is irrelevant to his claim to power. The communist leader can only legitimate himself by thinking and speaking more dialectically – that is, more paradoxically and totally – than any other person. Without this proof by language, legitimation would sooner or later be withdrawn from the leader.

But the aspiration to the kingdom of philosophy is integral to the definition of philosophy as such. After all, what basis could there be for thinking the world as a whole unless it be to govern this whole? To abolish philosophy's total claim to power is to abolish philosophy itself, leaving only the history of philosophy remaining. A common misconception must be dispelled here, however, one which also clouds our understanding of the Platonic state. To many, the call for the kingdom of philosophy sounds undemocratic, because philosophy is believed to be a specialized knowledge that most people do not possess. Thus it is assumed that the kingdom of philosophy means domination by an elite, a system of rule from which most people are excluded. Who is a philosopher, however? A philosopher is anyone who speaks, so long as he or she is speaking (or remaining eloquently silent), for all speech refers to the whole, directly or indirectly, and is in consequence philosophically relevant. Wittgenstein once attempted to cleanse everyday language of specifically philosophical language – that is to say, of language which refers to the whole, and which on that basis must be paradoxical – so that the public would become completely unphilosophical, and be permanently immunized from the dangers of the kingdom of philosophy. But as is well known, Wittgenstein did not succeed in this attempt. Instead, at the end of his life, he had to admit that philosophy is embedded too deeply within language itself (for Wittgenstein, this means that language itself is inherently too ill) for anyone who speaks to be able to avoid philosophizing, that is, to avoid referring to the whole of language in a paradoxical form. The attempt to eliminate this reference leads merely to a specific form of the kingdom of philosophy – one that is thoroughly perverted because self-destructive.

Another common misconception exists nowadays in which participation in language is understood as access to networks of communication where linguistic commodities circulate under the general conditions of the market. Resounding demands are made, again and again, that certain social, ethnic or other groups be allowed to communicate their claims through language by gaining access to these networks of communication. Such demands are undoubtedly legitimate, and should be welcomed. Yet this always still involves the linguistic representation of particular claims and interests. And, as a rule, these claims and demands are expressed clearly, explicitly and coherently so that they can ultimately enter into a compromise with other opposing claims. This is therefore a case of the expansion of sophistical discourse, not of uncovering the philosophical dimension of language. Firstly, these demands become commodities themselves, in that they begin to circulate through existing commercial networks of communication. And secondly, the inescapable internally contradictory nature of these demands is concealed, for the contradictions in question become compromises concluded in the medium of money. As information and communication, language loses its unity. It fragments into individually closed, coherent, and logically valid discourses that function on the market as commodities. And the only reason that these discourses remain coherent is that they project their contradictions onto the whole of capital, as they are paid to do. Rule by language cannot be established merely by demanding that individual and particular claims should be formulated in language in order to enable their access to pluralistic networks of communication. Establishing linguistic rule first requires uncovering and thematizing what is common and transindividual to all possible individual claims and ideas – that is, their inevitably paradoxical and self-contradictory logical structure.

Language can triumph over the economy only when it begins from the whole, with totality. The Soviet state was in this sense a form of the kingdom of philosophy. But the communist state can be distinguished from the Platonic state insofar as in the communist state it was the duty of every individual to be a philosopher, not just the duty of the governing class. The Soviet citizen could only satisfy his basic needs if he was recognized by the state as a philosophical thinker. This entailed that, every day, the citizen had to take the temperature of the whole of language in order to survive that day and the following night. This not only involved sensibility with respect to the development of political, ideological and cultural relations in the country itself, but it also involved, beyond this, a sensibility embracing the entire Earth. Someone who did not know how the Communist Party in Chile was faring that day, and what new and damaging adventures were being undertaken just then by American imperialism, risked receiving no new housing, no increase in salary and no permission for international travel. For those things one needed a recommendation from the local Party organization, which issued such a recommendation only when it judged that the Soviet citizen in question was genuinely Soviet, i.e., someone who thought sufficiently philosophically, placing his partial needs in the context of the whole.

Yet this demand to think and feel globally and with the whole of language was paradoxical insofar as it presupposed that the thought of the Soviet person in question was both Soviet and anti-Soviet at the same time. The correct responses to the questions posed would not be possible at all, that is, if the one being questioned were not very well informed indeed about which answers were regarded as anti-Soviet, for otherwise those answers could not be avoided. All Soviet discussions proceeded under the assumption either that all persons involved already thought in an anti-

Soviet way, or at a minimum that they knew precisely what it meant to think in an anti-Soviet way. Not coincidentally, official announcements of the period targeting anti-Soviet propaganda generally began with the words: 'Contrary to the well-known claims by x or y . . .', although these claims themselves were never officially made public. The communist leadership assumed, that is, either that everyone knew these claims already, or – corresponding to the total logic of dialectical materialism – that they could soon work them out for themselves. The principal demand placed on the Soviet person was therefore not that of Soviet thinking, but rather that of simultaneous Soviet and anti-Soviet thinking – thus that of total thought. For this reason, many of the ideologists of dialectical materialism were perplexed when in the Brezhnev era the first dissidents began publicly to proclaim 'truths' about the Soviet Union. At the time, one heard the constant refrain: but what these dissidents are saying has long been known already, everyone has always thought that, the texts of these dissidents are simply too naively constructed, too one-sided, too undialectical. Only subsequently was it noticed that it was precisely the undialectical quality of the dissident texts that integrated them into the wide-ranging media market of today's communication networks. The first market that emerged in the Soviet Union was the market in undialectical, formal-logically valid and coherent ideas – that is, the market in dissident and heretical ideas. But it is difficult for those who have once drunk the wine of totality to become accustomed to the market, including the media market. They are too drunk to recognize where their interests lie – indeed, they no longer truly have any. At some point they either forgot their interests, or lost them entirely; their interests have been left behind in a place that is no longer recognized.

In no sense, however, does the total linguistification of social being promise any quietening of social conflicts; on the contrary, it promises to intensify them. Under capitalist economic conditions, paradox can be interpreted as a conflict of interests, and thus it can be resolved, at least provisionally, by a compromise in the medium of money. In the medium of language, however, paradox can neither be paid off nor consequently disempowered. This entails that if communism is understood as the transcription of society into the medium of language, then it promises not an idyll but rather life in self-contradiction, a situation of the utmost internal division and tension. No idyll is discovered when, having once seen the effulgence of *logos*, the Platonic philosopher returns to the hell of human society. Stalin indirectly compares his dialectical materialism to the New Testament when he compares his opponents to textualists and Talmudists. In this way, he promises nothing but martyrdom to the *logos* become flesh – which in this case is the Communist Party and the Soviet people.

A passage from the *Short Course*, which refers in the following way to a text by Lenin, is particularly enlightening in this regard:

> Speaking of the materialist views of the ancient philosopher Heraclitus, who held that 'the world, the all in one, was not created by any god or any man, but was, is and ever will be a living flame, systematically flaring up and systematically dying down,' Lenin comments: 'A very good exposition of the rudiments of dialectical materialism.'[16]

Dialectical materialism is therefore an invitation to pass through the eternally living flame. And, as is generally known, only those who are themselves flames can pass through the flame unburnt. From the outset, this was never concealed from the communist masses. The most popular song from the period of the Civil War contains the following lines: 'Bravely we shall go into battle for the Soviet power/ And we shall all die to the last man in this fight.' This promise was kept. This was indeed what came to pass. The flame, ignited by the short-circuit of opposites, spread. Almost all received burns. Many were burnt to death. Then the eternally living flame died down – in its own time and until the next occasion.

16   *Short Course*, 112.

Chapter Three

Communism, from Outside Looking in

O nly very rarely was Soviet communism perceived from outside as a flame that had been ignited and kindled by logical paradox – as all-consuming life in self-contradiction. Outweighing this was the image of communism as an idyll organized by formal-logical and rational-technical means, and this held true for sympathizers of communism as much as for its opponents. When the question is asked whether or not the former state-socialist regimes of Eastern Europe should be regarded as communist, this is the perception that generally comes to mind. The overwhelming majority of the Western left holds the opinion that communist utopia was not realized but betrayed by these regimes. And the reason given in support of this is the total rationalization and bureaucratization of Soviet life. Rationalization is understood here in the sense of rule by instrumental, formal-logically organized, cold and inhuman reason. In short, 'actually existing' socialism is criticized for having sought to turn humans into automata, machines supposed to function according to a programme. What is genuinely human as such – consisting in the fact that a human is not only a rational thinking animal, but also an animal that desires – was thereby excluded and suppressed. No great distance separates the Western left and right in this assessment. Their difference consists only in that the right suspects an attack on the freedom of human desire in every utopia, because for the right the conflict between reason and emotion is inescapable and insurmountable, while the left believes in a 'true utopia' in the sense of a reconciliation or, at the least, a balance between reason and desire.

This perception of communism as an empire of cold rationality where humans are transformed into machines is shaped predominantly by the great literary tradition of utopian social blueprints and anti-utopian polemics, for in the Cold War period the West was denied an immediate experience of Soviet communism. This literary tradition runs from Plato, through Thomas More, Campanella, Saint-Simon and Fourier, to Zamyatin, Huxley and Orwell. The utopian society is described in this tradition, whether positively or negatively, as a thoroughly rationalized, functionalized and rigid society, in which all members have a clearly defined function, in which the entirety of their everyday life is strictly regulated, and in which a social programme that has been logically and minutely conceived and unambiguously stipulated rules out any deviation, both for society as a whole and for each of its members. But ruling out deviation in this way does not mean that deviation is actually forbidden.

Rather, deviation in a utopian society is unthinkable, because in such a society all members are equally enlightened; all think logically; all are capable of reaching an understanding of the rationally determined necessity of acting in this and in no other way. In the utopian society there is no compulsion except the compulsion of logic – and for this reason there are equally no rational grounds for deviating from the social programme. The *logos* that is embodied in such a utopian society is the contradiction-free, coherent rationalist *logos* of science – not the internally contradictory, paradoxical *logos* of philosophy.

Communist 'totalitarian' society is often described as a society that has been rationalistically organized through and through, as unlimited rule by logocentrism. This is particularly the case in critical and anti-utopian writings, where what is human as such is manifested in resistance to this rational order, in the ability to deviate from the socially predetermined programme. For modern anthropology, the position of humans does not lie between the animal and God, as was once the case, but rather between the animal and the machine. The authors of the older utopias tended to affirm what is mechanical in humans in order to differentiate humans more sharply from animals, for they perceived the greatest danger for humanity to lie in animality. By contrast, the authors of more modern anti-utopias have affirmed what is animal, passionate and instinctive in humans in order to differentiate them more sharply from machines, for they perceive a greater danger for humans in machinery than in animality. If this anthropology is accepted, then resistance to the compulsion of cold, mechanical logic can only come from the sources of the irrational – from beyond reason, from the empire of the feelings, which cannot be argued away and which remain immune to logic because they are innately ambivalent and contradictory. It is generally sexual desire – love – that inspires the heroes of anti-utopian novels to resist the compelling logic of a thoroughly rationalized utopian society. Theoretical writings that target the utopian social project basically mount the same fundamental argument as do anti-utopian novels. Nietzsche appeals to the human yearning for death when he wishes to ironize the ideal of a secure existence in a perfect society. Bataille writes about excess, Eros and the festival as sources of sovereignty – sources which communist society may seek to dry up in the name of the rational organization of the social production process, but which it cannot.

Arguments against utopian projects therefore generally take the form of arguing in the name of ambivalent desire against the rule of mechanical, coherent and contradiction-free rationality. They seek to demonstrate that humans are not only bearers of logic, but also creatures who are possessed by feelings that are irrational because they are contradictory. And this entails that the elimination of social contradictions through the realization of a utopian project cannot succeed, because the basis for these contradictions lies deeper than reason – in human nature itself, which is akin to animal nature. If logic is understood as a system of rules of universal validity, then logic must collapse in the face of human nature, for each human is singular in his or her inner contradictoriness and cannot be subsumed as an individual case under a general rule. And this entails further that anyone who strives for the realization of utopia must fight against what is human as such. Either what is human is thus destroyed, or utopia is destroyed by what is human. Every rationalist utopianism proves to be hostile to human beings because it wishes to kill the animal in the human and turn the human into a machine. Now, Soviet communism, regarded from this perspective, appears as a particularly radical form of rationalist modernity – and in this radicality, one that is also particularly naive and brutal. In Western films dating from the Cold War in which communists from the East are represented, it is striking that communists generally appear as robots, as spectres, as inhuman, internally empty, bodiless machines.

The best metaphor for the Western perception of the communist human image is to be found in the film *Invasion of the Body Snatchers* and its various remakes.[17] The

17   1956, directed by Don Siegel; 1977, directed by Philip Kaufmann; 1992, directed by Abel Ferrara.

totalitarian, thoroughly rationalized society is established in this film through the partial de-corporealization of humans. The human appearance, the surfaces of the human form, are retained. But it is a case here of an empty shell: the interior, the human flesh as such, is absent. In consequence, all the contradictory instincts, desires and emotions that could have afforded resistance to totalitarian control are also lacking. The sub-corporeal fleshless humans are completely at the mercy of utopian reason because they lack the obscure forces of desire and the animal vitality of revolt that are required to resist mechanical rationality. The inhabitants of utopia – or of the 'Matrix', if you will – are just such sub-corporeal, partially dematerialized, virtualized people. Derrida states nothing contrary to this in his book *Specters of Marx*, written after the downfall of Eastern European communism.[18] To characterize the intramundane appearance of communism, Derrida takes up the metaphor from *The Communist Manifesto* of communism as a spectre – a spectre haunting all of world history. Derrida compares the spectre of communism to the ghost of Hamlet's father as described by Shakespeare. Those who observe this ghost see only his outside, the surfaces, the armour, but do not know what is hidden beneath this. Above all, it is not known

18   Jacques Derrida, *Specters of Marx*, trans. Peggy Kamuf, New York and London: Routledge, 1994, 4ff.

whether there really is anything hidden beneath, or whether the ghost is not actually internally empty – a pure signifier without signified, without flesh, without desire. To external observers, Soviet communism clearly did not appear as an incarnation of communist utopia, but rather as a continued haunting by the communist spectre – an impression that can probably be attributed to its formulaic, ritualized and well-rehearsed appearance. Even when citing *The Communist Manifesto* or *Hamlet*, Derrida's description of communism is most reminiscent of the film *Body Snatchers*. In this account, the spectre of communism was and remains never truly incarnated. It lacks flesh: it can do no more than haunt. The reality of communism has no depths; it is a case of a merely mediating surface.

This Western perception of Eastern communism cannot be explained exclusively by the fact that Western intellectuals escaped coming into bodily contact with communism due to the fronts of the Cold War. Eastern communist propaganda of the period also powerfully assisted in the development of this perception. Communist leaders portrayed themselves as pre-programmed automata who, with rigid faces and in an entirely unironic manner, performed incomprehensible rituals or issued boring statements drearily and formulaically. Nor was this image altered in the slightest by the fact that the Communist Party was particularly active and influential in France. For the French communists similarly presented themselves as 'snatched' – as figures whose flesh had been stolen. Their language was just as ossified and tautological, becoming the *langue du bois*. But the concrete historical reasons for this perception of Soviet communism as the empire of automata, of virtualized, sub-corporeal spectre-people, are less important here than the fact itself: in the West, the Cold War between East and West was principally stylized as a struggle between bodies and machines, between feelings and cold rationality, between desire and logic, between love and rationalist utopia. It was for this reason that the CIA supported exhibitions by Pollock and other abstract expressionists: their paintings functioned as manifestations of quasi-animalistic revolt against the cold logic of rationalist utopia. It was for this reason too that sensuous Western luxury won out over the cold ascetic logic of the Russian commissar in the most famous film of the Cold War, Ernst Lubitsch's *Ninotchka*. The entire history of the Cold War is basically summed up best by the old joke: *ex oriente lux, ex occidente luxus*.

This observation is significant because it allows for a better understanding of the genealogy of the critique of logocentrism, of the rule of cold rationality, which is positioned today as a leftist critique of the institutions of capitalist society. This critique was originally 'anti-totalitarian', that is, it was directed against the opponent of the West in the Cold War, against the Soviet Union. With time, however, it was increasingly employed against the institutions of the West itself, which were perceived in their turn as cold, rationalistic, calculating and inhuman – i.e., in a certain sense, as 'totalitarian'. This discourse is therefore a critique of Soviet communism that has been repurposed as a self-critique of the West. In the process, the anti-communist genealogy of this discourse has generally been forgotten or, better put, repressed. And yet this genealogy is nonetheless of decisive significance for the functioning of the discourse about desire, for every society is prepared to accept a critique that has already demonstrated its effectiveness in the struggle against that society's opponent. The development undergone by the figure of Big Brother is characteristic in this respect. Big Brother was originally devised by Orwell to parody the Soviet political system. But with time, it began to function as a description for any surveillance state. And because the technological possibilities for surveillance are best developed in the West, this figure is now used most frequently to characterize the security mania of Western states. A critique of this kind appears to be very radical, but it has the advantage of not calling the borders of the Cold War into question, and this remains so today even though the Cold War is now long over. As it currently functions in the West, critical discourse thus proves to be astonishingly homogeneous. It is always the same things being criticized with the same arguments. The only difference consists in that the right tends to apply this critique to the non-West (communism and now Islam are principally criticized as ideologies that oppress the body and sexuality), while the left conversely practises this same critique as a self-critique of the West – and, from the middle, the same critique is applied in both directions, as a fair-minded 'both . . . and also . . .', albeit in a moderated form.

This astounding and historically unparalleled homogeneity of Western critical discourse, which never changes its components but merely alters its direction now and then, certainly cannot be explained solely by the ideological pressure imposed on the Western public sphere during the Cold War period. Instead, this homogeneity can be attributed principally to the fact that critical discourse in the West circulates primarily as a commodity on the media market. It is a standardized and sophistical mode of speech available for employment by any political strategy whatsoever. After all, where is the body not suppressed? Where are people not traumatized? Where is the subject who is not seized by contradictory desires? Where is the human not threatened by the machine? The answer is that this is the case everywhere. The sales potential of this critique is therefore potentially infinite. In addition, the discourse of desire suits the market well in terms of content, for it represents an intermediary station on the path that the different religions, ideologies and sciences take towards their successful commercialization.

As soon as an ideology or religion ceases to talk about 'spirit' and translates its dusty conceptual apparatus into the language of desire, it immediately becomes marketable. In a certain sense, dialectical materialism itself was already a step in this direction. But the decisive role here belongs to Alexandre Kojève who, in his famous seminar on Hegel's *Phenomenology of Spirit* held in Paris between 1933 and 1939, transformed the history of the Hegelian absolute spirit into the history of desire (*désir*) – the contradictory desire for the desire of the other. It is particularly easy to recognize Kojève's influence in Lacan and Bataille, who belonged to the closest circle of his students, with Bataille going furthest along the path of the theoretical economization of desire. Kojève himself is known to have favoured a practical solution to the problem and, after the interruption of his seminar by the war, moved directly into formulating economic policy in post-war Europe.

The extreme homogeneity of standard Western critical discourse is often overlooked, especially when the absence of critical discourse in non-Western states is being bemoaned. In such cases the old spectre of (anti-)communism enjoys a spectral resurrection. The citizens of states that have not adopted the Western model of democracy are regarded as preferring blind obedience to the free expression of opinions; they lack the courage to deal with social conflicts openly; they instead call for authority, and so on. Or in other words, the absence of democracy is attributed to their need for social homogeneity. To remedy this situation, pluralism, an open society and the recognition of heterogeneity and differences are prescribed. In most cases – although certainly not in all – this is a misdiagnosis. There are indeed societies in the world that are pre-modern insofar as they understand themselves as traditional communities (*Gemeinschaften*) and not as modern societies (*Gesellschaften*), to employ a common terminology. Such communities are so homogeneous – or rather understand themselves to be so homogeneous – that they believe they do not require the institutions of pluralistic Western-style democracy. The charge of not having gone far enough along in the process of internal differentiation can be justly levelled against these societies.

But such traditional 'closed' societies should not be confused with societies of a completely different type, in which social differentiation has proceeded to such an extent that they can no longer be held together by means of democratic mediation. These societies are so internally divided and contradictory that they are no longer capable of consensus in the spirit of classical formal-logical validity – that consensus for which Western-style democratic process strives. Only a government whose thoughts and actions are internally contradictory can satisfy these extreme contradictions and divisions. Such a society may come together in agreement – but it agrees on the internal contradiction, on paradox.

Here differentiation has not failed to appear, but has instead gone too far. One hesitates to describe such societies simply as post-democratic, for it is not immediately obvious that the possibility of consensus and thus of a transition to democracy along Western lines has been ruled out forever. But in any case, such extremely heterogeneous societies constitute another variant of modernity – one could even say its extreme variant. This variant takes on significance above all when considered from a global rather than a national perspective, for the regulation or overcoming of globally operating contradictions by a global agreement of humanity with itself can hardly be said to be possible. Nor should it be forgotten that the Platonic state arose precisely as a design for a post-democratic kingdom of philosophy, which was supposed to prove itself capable of administering all those divisions and contradictions that democracy was not in a position to eliminate.

Admittedly, politics is generally understood nowadays not as the administration of the *polis*, as it is described for instance in Plato's *Republic*, but rather as action in an open, agonistic and heterogeneous social field. The closure of such an open political field by an administration, even if it be an administration that thinks and acts dialectically, accordingly appears tantamount to the abolition of politics. On this basis, political theory of recent decades has tended to thematize the irreducible heterogeneity of different political discourses and practices such that any agreement between them must be considered as a false agreement. Such political theory is not even prepared to accept that type of agreement about difference which is called, in political jargon, 'agreement to disagree'. This is why a rigorous advocate of openness will avoid defining the political field in rigid oppositions. Instead of this, he will not only place in question the possibility of any genuine agreement between the conflicting parties, but also question the very possibility of an agreement of each of the conflicting parties with itself. Ultimately, the heterogeneity of the political field can be guaranteed only by the non-identity of the political forces that shape this field. Each individual political discourse, and similarly every individual political praxis, must be understood in such a way that it contradicts itself, that it cannot guarantee its own identity, that it becomes lost in paradox and ambivalence, that it deconstructs itself. Only then does the political field become radically heterogeneous, and incapable of closure in principle. It is just like Hollywood films with an open ending: the villain disappears in the night, the hero rides out towards the rising sun. Batman forever. Democracy after democracy. Justice follows upon justice. One waits for the next film.

In this infinite perspective of political openness and heterogeneity, Soviet communism clearly does not look good. Its claim to a definitive political victory, and to the concomitant total administration of society in the spirit of its own political theory, appears instead to be a betrayal of the real task of the communist movement, which consists in struggling ever further for the oppressed, the disadvantaged and the exploited – and thus proceeding ever further into the free space of its own ambiguities, uncertainties and contradictions. But as stated above, Soviet communism in no way denies its own contradictoriness, which it shares with all other discourses. And nonetheless – or precisely because of this – dialectical materialism considers itself to be superior to all other discourses. It knows itself to be capable, that is, of grasping what is common to all discourses – the commonality that these discourses themselves overlook. Dialectical materialism does not look for what is common to all discourses at the point where they could potentially be brought to agreement. The inescapability of class conflict alone is sufficient to prove such agreement to be impossible. Rather, it locates this common ground at the point where all discourses contradict not only other discourses but also themselves. Dialectical materialism is a theory about the inner contradictoriness of all things and all discourses, including itself. The contradictory, paradoxical character of every discourse thus presents dialectical materialism with the possibility of administering the field of all discourses without homogenizing that field. In this way, dialectical materialism provides the subject with the chance to appropriate and administer this paradoxical, ambivalent and heterogeneous field without lapsing into one-sidedness in the process. Admittedly, this presumes that the oppositions that lead to paradox not only cannot be overcome and sublated, but also cannot be deconstructed. And indeed, if all oppositions were dissolved through an infinite labour of deconstruction, then no further contradictions or paradoxes could arise. But the reason why such an infinite labour of deconstruction cannot be accomplished de facto is easy to comprehend. The political field can certainly be thought of as infinitely heterogeneous. But it is infinitely heterogeneous only in the imagination, only virtually. Materially, it is always finite. And it is finite because capital is finite.

Modern capitalist society is defined by the fact that the things in it are as they are because there is not enough money to fashion them differently. And indeed, if today one visits the home of an acquaintance, or a school, a church, or a bar, and asks why it is that what one sees is the way it is and not otherwise, one invariably receives the answer that it has long been planned to arrange things completely differently – in ways that are better and more modern and on a higher level of efficiency, technological progress and cutting-edge design – but that unfortunately the money for this is still lacking. This is why what is remains the way it is for the time being – until the money arrives that will allow everything to be re-made anew. The reason why things are finite, why they are present at all, why they have a form, why they are offered to the gaze of the observer as these concrete objects, is because they are under-financed. If their finance were infinite, they would be constantly changed, improved, 'updated', modernized – and thus de-corporealized. Infinite finance would transform the entire world into a Deleuzian body without organs, in which all things would become completely fluid and immaterial. In capitalist society, money plays the same role as time in the philosophy of Heidegger. According to Heidegger, everything that exists is the way it is because it lacks the time to become otherwise. But time, as has long been known, is really money. In capitalism, the formative power of capital is manifested through its absence, through under-financing.

In order for differences and heterogeneities to become ever more different and more heterogeneous in an infinite conflict, one likewise needs money for conferences, symposia, projects and publications that are financed by different foundations. As many differences and heterogeneities, as many cultural and sexual identities, as there is finance. It is precisely the same as with sub-atomic particles. On the one hand, sub-atomic particles are primary because all matter is made up of them. But in relation to finance they are secondary, because the greater the acceleration that releases the sub-atomic particles by splitting matter, the more sub-atomic particles are discovered – and the size of the particle accelerator depends entirely upon its finance. Although in modernity, creativity is celebrated as the origin of all things, the actual form of all things is due not to creativity but to their limitation, their interruption, their closure by under-financing. The world is said to have come into being when God retired to rest on the seventh day. Had God shown infinite creativity, we would still be waiting today for the results.

Nor should the openness of a society be measured by the access its members have to networks of communication, the extent of which is necessarily finite. While it is certainly true that if someone enjoys communicating with other people, then he is said in everyday life to be an open person, to be open can also mean to be divided. Thus a wound can be described as open because it opens the body. In this sense one can be alone, isolated, non-communicative – and at the same time be internally divided, non-identical and open. The subject of dialectical materialism is open because his thought is divided, paradoxical and heterogeneous. And one can also speak of openness with regard to a communist subject ruling in an isolated country. The internal division, and the internal tension to which this division gives rise, even allow openness to become manifest much more clearly in the thinking of a solitary and finite subject than in the bad, undialectical infinity of a boring repetition of ever-same communication, the work of difference and the establishment of heterogeneity. Infinite communication does not open the subject, but rather automatizes, tautologizes and trivializes it. The open subject instead comes into being by appropriating the open and divided field of language as his own, dividing himself and making himself paradoxical and heterogeneous. Such an open subject is at the same time a revolutionary subject.

The bourgeois left, by contrast, which bemoans the restriction of the heterogeneous political field by the capitalist market, may well be critical of capitalism, but it is not revolutionary. It protests against the market because it thinks that the market homogenizes the heterogeneous and closes down openness with its finite, rational calculations. The left instead wishes to defend infinite heterogeneity, the infinite work of difference, the incalculable, the uneconomizable and radical otherness against the power of the market. This intention is undoubtedly good and noble, and yet, expressed in orthodox Marxist language, it is 'idealist'. It is idealist not in the sense of a 'metaphysical' opposition between mind and matter – an opposition which needs to be deconstructed – but rather because it strives for an infinity that cannot be materialized, made real, incarnated. Its reference to infinity entails that the anti-capitalist critique remains at best a mere critique – a critique that, for its part, thereby becomes infinite, repetitive and tautological. At worst, it changes such a critique into an apologia for the market.

In the period of the feudal *ancien régime*, reference to the divine hierarchies that stretched heavenwards infinitely high above the worldly hierarchies was certainly critical with regard to those worldly hierarchies, for worldly power was thereby relativized. But at the same time, this reference was also an apologia, for worldly hierarchies could be interpreted quite simply as finite fragments of the infinite divine hierarchies, and thereby infinitely legitimated. The same thing occurs with reference to the infinite play of signifiers or the infinite work of difference. The finite market is criticized because it is finite. Above all, the market is criticized because it creates winners and losers, because it presents individuals with the chance not only to succeed but also to fail. Under capitalist market conditions, difference transforms into competition. Thus the infinite unfolding of differences is given determinate boundaries. This restriction is even affirmed by some of the so-called 'neoliberal' thinkers. Karl Popper, who first minted the concept of the open society, popularized it and used it to attack Plato, Hegel and Marx, likewise introduced the chance of definitive failure into scientific theory. According to Popper, a theory certainly cannot be definitively proven true, but it can be definitively disproven if it is established that certain facts speak against it. Similarly, a company can never definitively succeed in the open market, but it can definitively fail. Similarly too, a discourse can fail definitively in the market of discourses. For the advocates of infinite openness and heterogeneity, this possibility of definitive failure is frightening. For in the infinite perspective of the infinite work of differences, no definitive failure is possible. There, as in the paradise of the old religions, all differences remain different. It is in this sense that Derrida speaks of deconstruction as ultimate justice. This is a case of messianic, divine justice that compensates for every worldly failure through the infinite work of difference – whereby worldly differentiation, as a fragment of the infinite work of difference, is both criticized and further deconstructed, but also accepted. The irreducible, unhomogenizable, infinite, virtual empire of heterogeneities and differences is actually nothing but bourgeois pluralism without market losers, capitalism as utopia, the market in a state of paradise. In orthodox Marxist language, this is clearly a matter of a neo-theological opiate of the people – this time, admittedly, an opiate for intellectual people, for those who would like to keep on fostering their differences to infinity.

By contrast, the revolutionary subject operates not with differentiations, but with commands, prohibitions and decrees. The language of the revolutionary subject is purely performative. The credibility of this language arises solely from its paradoxicality. In this, the revolutionary subject most strongly resembles the artist, whose language is likewise purely performative. The artist does not give reasons for his art, nor does he explain it. He acts in the open – as one who opens. To make art means to decree that things should be thus and not otherwise – and without any 'objective' basis. Of course, this does not mean that in art 'anything goes'. Art praxis is only recognized as such if it is paradoxical. If an artwork looks like art, then it is regarded not as art but as kitsch. If art looks like non-art, then it is simply non-art. In order to be recognized as art, art should look like art and simultaneously like non-art. This is clearly a demand that can be realized only in practice. Also essential to this act of realization is the decision at some point to make an end, to cease work on the artwork – and certainly not because finance for it is lacking, but rather because the artwork would lose its paradoxical character were work on it to continue infinitely long. Without the possibility of a cessation of art praxis, no art can come into being. This observation serves to clarify why the cessation of the project of communism likewise does not mean the betrayal of communism.

Chapter Four

The Kingdom of Philosophy:
The Administration of Metanoia

W hy did the communist parties of the East – first and foremost the Soviet and the Chinese Communist Parties – cease work on the communist project and instead switch their countries to the development of capitalism? This question can only be answered properly when examined in the context of the materialist dialectic. As has been stated, the materialist dialectic thinks the unity of A and not-A. If A is a project, then not-A is the context of this project. To impel project A ever onwards is to act one-sidedly, because the context of this project, namely not-A, is then ignored forever. Moreover, the context of such a project becomes its fate, for this context dictates the conditions within which the project is to be realized. Passing from the project to its context is a necessity for anyone who seeks to grasp the whole. And because the context of Soviet communism was capitalism, the next step in the realization of communism had to be the transition from communism to capitalism. The project of building communism in a single country is not refuted by this transition, but is instead confirmed and definitively realized. For communism is thus given a historical location not just in space but also in time; that is to say, it becomes a complete historical formation with the possibility of even being reproduced or repeated.

The principal problem of a society that understands itself as an open society is that of limiting its projects, of bringing them to an end. In such a society it is well-nigh impossible to consider a project as finite. In an open society, economic growth, scientific research and the struggle for social justice can only be conceived of as infinite; so too desire, and the work of difference. Whatever limits are set for the realization of these projects are dictated solely by the 'objective' conditions within which they are developed and made real. In an open society, projects are thus realized only to the extent that they are interrupted at some point from outside. As discussed above, under-financing is the primary cause for projects being halted at some point and thereby finally receiving a form, that is, being realized. Generational change is the other reason for the cessation of projects: the protagonists of a project die out, the new generation loses interest and the project falls out of fashion. Projects are constantly becoming 'outdated' in this sense instead of being realized. The life of an open modern society has a rhythm that is determined almost entirely by biology. Each generation has a certain period of time at its disposal, generally around a decade, in which to formulate and develop its projects. Of course work on these projects may subsequently continue. But all that is thought and done in such cases will be regarded as outdated and irrelevant by definition. In an open society, economics and biology thus discharge the function of limiting, bringing to end and incarnating projects that would otherwise never receive a form, a body.

Hence limits to the projective infinity of thought – to what Hegel termed bad infinity – are set in open societies as well. So the question is not whether closure actually occurs, for it occurs in every case, but rather when and how this closure occurs. In an open capitalist society, closure is predominantly administered by capital. By contrast, philosophy has always aimed to appropriate and administer this event of closure, limitation, interruption and transition itself, and not to allow it to be externally dictated. A project can also be brought to an end by a deliberate shift of perspective from the project itself to the context of this project. In the philosophical tradition, such a change of perspective is termed metanoia. The term metanoia can be used to describe the transition from an individual subjective perspective to a general perspective, to a metaposition. Metanoia is also used in the sense of a conversion to the Christian faith, which similarly changes the perspective from which the world is regarded. Husserl's call for a phenomenological reduction, in which the 'natural attitude' is replaced by the 'phenomenological attitude', is likewise a call for metanoia. The famous formula of McLuhan, 'the medium is the message' is also a de facto demand for metanoia – the shift of attention from the message to its medium. However, metanoia need not be performed in only one direction. Having attained the universal perspective of the good as such, Plato posed the question of how ideas of the good could be embodied in the intramundane state. Husserl asks how the disposition for the phenomenological reduction is to be located historically. If metanoia is the transition from the object to its context, then there is also a reversed metanoia, which asks about the context of that context, thus leading back to the earlier perspective at a different level of reflection.

It is often claimed nowadays that the conquest of a metaposition is impossible, and that metanoia is thus similarly impossible: one's original perspective cannot be changed at will. The possibility of metanoia appears to be based solely in metaphysics, that is, in the privileging of the soul in relation to the body. But if there is no immortal soul that can transcend the finite body, then obtaining a metaposition also appears to be impossible, for the body always has a particular structure and location in the world that dictate a person's perspective and cannot be changed arbitrarily. This argument was advanced with particular vehemence by Nietzsche, and it has subsequently almost acquired the status of a self-evident proposition, so that whenever anyone speaks today, he is afterwards asked first about where he comes from and from which perspective he speaks. Race, class and gender serve as the standard coordinates of this space in which each speaker is inherently positioned. The concept of cultural identity also serves this same goal of initial positioning. The effectiveness of these parameters is barely diminished even when they are interpreted not as 'natural' determinants but as social constructions. For while social constructions can be deconstructed, they cannot be abolished, altered or exchanged at will. Hence the only options available to the subject are those either of infinitely cultivating the cultural identity pregiven by his body (or by the social codification of this body), or of infinitely deconstructing this identity. In Hegelian terms, however, both infinities are bad infinities, for it is not known how they can be limited and brought to an end. One can only hope that this reflection on one's own perspective ceases at some point because the money required for continuing it any further has run out. Or alternatively, hope that death will finally arrive some day, and one will no longer be bothered by questions of the type 'where do you come from', because another question will have become more important, that of where we have gone.

But there is no such thing as a perfect synchronization of body and soul. Classical metaphysics anticipated the life of the soul after the end of the body. Metanoia, understood as the transition from the usual, worldly 'natural' perspective to an alternative, universal and metaphysical perspective, entailed the abstraction from one's own worldly perspective in expectation of the continued life of the soul following the death of the body. Today, metanoia functions as the anticipation of the continued life of the body as a corpse following the death of the soul. Hence, even given the presuppositions of the most rigorous materialism, it is possible to alter one's perspective through metanoia prior to the change of perspective being externally dictated by economics or biology. Metanoia, that is, is not only possible when humans are understood as being under-incarnated – i.e., not only when one's soul is supposed to outlast the body – but also when humans are understood as being over-incarnated, as is the case in the modern era – i.e., when it is thought that the soul lives more briefly than the body. Following the end of the soul, the body is transported to a different place from the one in which it was located during its life – namely, to the cemetery. Foucault quite rightly includes the cemetery along with the museum, the clinic, the prison and the ship (and one could also add the rubbish heap) amongst those other places, the heterotopias. Thus a human can experience metanoia by imagining his or her body as a corpse during life, thereby acquiring a heterotopian perspective.

Deconstruction can also be understood as an effect of such an 'other' metanoia – as the thematization of a postmortal decomposition that has 'always already' begun in life. The same can be said of the Deleuzian 'body without organs', which is likewise best envisaged as a corpse in an advanced state of decomposition. And this also holds true for the mass-cultural interest in figures that symbolize the continued life of the body after the death of the soul: vampires, zombies and so on. For our purposes, what is most important to emphasize here is that metanoia, which is indispensible for gaining access to the whole, does not stand in contradiction to the principal thesis of materialism concerning the impossibility of the continued life of the soul after death. Metanoia not only anticipates the limiting and ending of bad infinity by nature or economics; it simultaneously accelerates this process of bringing to an end. This acceleration of the transition, compared to the 'natural' or 'economic' transition, is of decisive importance for any politics. The administration of metanoia establishes the possibility of being quicker than time. It involves a type of asceticism of time: one gives oneself less time than nature or the economy would have placed at one's disposal.

Asceticism generally consists in allowing oneself less than is allowed by external factors. In no sense does this entail internalizing from a feeling of weakness those limits that have been set externally. In describing asceticism as such an act of internalization, Nietzsche overlooked its most important dimension. Asceticism does not consist in passively accepting the limits that are forced on us from outside; it consists rather in drawing those limits much closer than is necessary. Only by imposing these more narrow limits on one's own possibilities can sovereignty, authorship and autonomy be won. Modern art is often characterized as a series of broken taboos, as a constant expansion of the possibility of making art. In fact, the situation is precisely the reverse. New taboos and new reductions were constantly being introduced in modern art. For no obvious reason, artists imposed on themselves the obligation to use only abstract geometric figures, or only ready-mades, or only words. The forms of modern art are due solely to this self-imposed ascetic creation of taboos, restrictions and reductions. This example demonstrates that newness arises not from expansion but rather from reduction, from a new mode of asceticism. Metanoia leads to a renunciation – namely the renunciation of always doing the same thing, of always following the same path, always seeking to ride out further in the same bad infinity. Badiou speaks about fidelity to the revolutionary event.[19] But fidelity to revolution is fidelity to infidelity. The asceticism of time entails the duty of being unfaithful, of bringing about the transition, the change, the metanoia even when – indeed

19   Alain Badiou, *Metapolitics*, trans. Jason Barker, London and New York: Verso, 2005, 127ff.

precisely when – there are no external circumstances that compel this metanoia upon us.

An insight central to Hegel is relevant here: thinking is defined by the incessant alternation of thoughts. It was on this basis that Hegel regarded with extreme scepticism the intention of remaining faithful to one's own ideas and thoughts. And indeed, even if someone represents a political viewpoint so consistently that he never expresses or accepts a contrary view, this still does not entail that he always remains faithful to his political viewpoint. For sometimes he will also think about other things, such as eating, sleeping, or other everyday activities. But then he is thinking of what is other to his political ideas, of the not-A, of the context within which he articulates his views. Hence he also accepts the status quo, and this itself includes a political dimension – and indeed, a political dimension that possibly contradicts de facto the political viewpoint to which he wishes to remain faithful. To think means nothing other than constantly to alter the thoughts one has 'in one's head'. Not by chance, Hegel discusses how the revolutionary guillotine is a true portrayal of thinking because it causes heads to roll approximately as fast as thoughts rotate in those heads.[20] Hegel sought to introduce a logic – dialectical logic, to be precise – into

20 Georg Wilhelm Friedrich Hegel, *Phenomenology of Spirit*, trans. A.V. Miller, Oxford: Clarendon Press, 1977, 359ff.

this process of the alternation of thoughts, but we can agree with Kierkegaard that such a logic is ultimately arbitrary. There is simply no unequivocal criterion for determining if a project or an ideology or a religion 'has outlived itself', 'is historically superseded'. We remain trapped in paradox and cannot merely rely on the course of time to resolve it for us. Metanoia remains ultimately groundless, purely performative, revolutionary.

For Hegel, the world is the way it is as the product of this dialectical reversal, the repeated metanoia of the absolute spirit. But at some point this constant self-renunciation of the absolute spirit must itself have become absolute, compelling the spirit to be silent, to stop. For Hegel, reality has been abandoned by spirit: it is what is left over after the history of spirit. When spirit is no longer present, the dialectic also appears to stop, and relations stabilize. By contrast, dialectical materialism has relocated the contradictions into the things themselves, into bodies, into what is material. Even when the soul has abandoned the body, the body's exchanges with its environment do not cease – they merely take on a different form. The quantitative becomes the qualitative – but the whole dialectical process does not thereby stop. Where the soul once was has now become corpse. But the difference, if this difference is considered dialectically, is not so great as it may appear at first glance.

The Soviet regime was above all the administration of metanoia, of constant transition, of constant endings and new beginnings, of self-contradiction. Lenin's corpse, which was and remains exhibited in a mausoleum, is the immutable icon of materialist metanoia, of the permanent change practised by the Soviet communist leadership. Change is anti-utopian: if utopia is understood to be a definitive, perfectly rational order, then change is a betrayal of utopia. But when change ceases to be blind change driven by nature or by the forces of capitalism, then it acquires a dimension of grace. Change is thereby linguistified, becoming metanoia – and in consequence the possibility arises of speaking to this change, of criticizing it, of addressing complaints to it. Both Lenin and Stalin and later Mao all used their power constantly to re-ignite the revolution and administer it anew. They wished always to be more dialectical than history itself, to pre-empt time. Their greatest fear was of being too late, of missing the moment that calls for change. This desire for the turning point, for the new beginning, also gripped the Soviet Union following the death of Stalin, shortly after which massive de-Stalinization commenced. Even public reference to the name of Stalin was forbidden, or at least reduced to a minimum; Stalin's writings became inaccessible; his deeds were expunged from the history books. Then came the Brezhnev era of so-called stagnation. This period was basically the Soviet version of the *belle époque*; people began to grow bored. The Party reacted to this growing boredom with the Stalinist slogans of reconstruction and acceleration (*perestroika i uskorenie*). As in the Stalin era, reconstruction, change or metanoia was understood and practised as the path to acceleration. Once again, the intention was to be faster than history, faster than time.

Although the self-abolition of communism at the initiative and under the direction of the leadership of the Communist Party is a historically unique event, it is often trivialized because it is still consistently styled as a defeat in a war – in this instance, the Cold War – or as the result of the struggle for freedom by the peoples subjugated by communism. But neither of these very familiar explanations is accurate. The Cold War was not a war, but only a metaphor of a war: it was therefore a war that could only be lost metaphorically. In military terms, the Soviet Union was unassailable. And all those groups that had spoken out for their freedom had been entirely pacified prior to the transition to capitalism. The Russian dissident movement had been wholly finished off, until the mid-1980s. The *Solidarność* movement in Poland had been brought to an end just as promptly by the Polish security forces. The unrest in Beijing was successfully suppressed, and order was restored. It was precisely this total defeat of every internal opposition and this complete immunity with regards to any possible external intervention that led the Soviet and the Chinese leaderships to undertake the transition to capitalism. If either leadership had not felt absolutely secure, it would never have undertaken such immense reconstruction and acceleration.

The fact that the Soviet Union disintegrated in the course of this reconstruction has sometimes contributed to this perception of a defeat. The Soviet Union was regarded from outside predominantly as the 'Russian empire', and its disintegration is consequently often interpreted as the defeat of Russia in its struggle against the efforts of other nations for independence. Somehow it is forgotten here that it was in fact Russia that dismantled the Soviet Union, when the Russian government – at the time under Yeltsin – withdrew from the Soviet Union in an agreement with the Ukraine and Belorussia. Independence was thus imposed on the other Soviet Republics. It was a turning point that was induced from above, from the centre, at the initiative of a leadership that had been raised in the conviction that its task consisted in shaping history dialectically, not in suffering it passively. Marxists have always believed that capitalism represents the best mechanism for economic acceleration. Marx frequently emphasized this, and employed it as an argument against 'utopian communism'. The proposal to tame capitalism, to instrumentalize it, to set it to work within the frame of a socialist order and under the control of the Communist Party for communist victory – this had been on the agenda from the October Revolution on. It was a possibility that was much discussed, and had even been tested from time to time, although only very inconsistently. However, the idea had never been finally translated into action because the communist leadership had never felt secure enough, and feared losing power through this experiment. In the 1980s and '90s, it felt strong enough, and risked the experiment. It is still too soon to judge whether this experiment has failed. In China, the Communist Party is still firmly in control. In Russia, central control is continually being strengthened, rather than being weakened. The model will be tested further – and may yet prove entirely successful.

In this context, it is worth recalling that both the conditions and the juridical process for the disintegration of the Soviet Union were actually designed and created by Stalin. In the so-called 'Stalinist Constitution' of 1936, Article 17 states: 'Each Union Republic shall retain the right freely to secede from the USSR.' This formulation was later adopted without any alteration in the final Soviet Constitution of 1977 as Article 72. The significance of this Article is made sufficiently clear when it is recalled that the only civil war in the history of the USA was sparked by this question of whether the individual states were free to leave the union. The individual Republics, by contrast, were constitutionally guaranteed the right to withdraw without any restrictions or conditions. This shows that the Soviet Union was conceived by Stalin from the outset not as a unified state but as a loose union of independent states. The objection that such a constitution pre-programmes a potential disintegration of the Soviet Union was already raised at the time by certain experts in international law. Stalin, however, was steadfast in his decision to retain the Article in question unchanged. The reason for this could only be that Stalin wanted to define the Soviet Union dialectically – as at once state and non-state.

No doubt, the Stalinist constitution inherited this definition from still earlier documents of union. But its retention can only be interpreted as a response to criticism directed against Stalin's thesis of the possibility of building socialism in one country – most notably, criticism by Trotsky. This country, in which socialism was to be built, was therefore presented as a federation of nations, as a collection of countries – more of a socialist community of states, standing in opposition to the capitalist community of states, than a single, unitary and isolated state. In the Soviet Union this conception of a community of states was also carried out consistently in everyday life. Each Republic had its government, its parliament, its administration, its language. There were official visits of party and state functionaries from one Republic to another; conferences of writers were organized, as were cultural festivals, exchanges of experts, and so on. The internal life of the state was performed as if on an international stage. But the decisive role in all this was played by the category 'nationality' in the passport of every Soviet citizen. The function of this category was and remains a mystery to foreigners, who understand nationality to mean citizenship of a state. But it played an important role for all citizens of the Soviet Union – and indeed, in all spheres of their lives. There, nationality meant membership of a people, ethnic origin. One could choose one's nationality only if one's parents were of different nationalities. Otherwise, the nationality of the parents was inherited. In every practical matter – and above all when looking for work – one was asked about one's nationality, and often about the nationality of one's parents. Thus Soviet internationalism did not mean a one-sided universalism that would overcome and efface ethnic differences. To the contrary, in the construction of the Soviet Union as a socialist and internationalist community of states, none of its citizens were allowed ever to forget where they came from. Only the Communist Party, embodying dialectical reason, could decide where nationality ended and where internationalism began, and vice versa.

The process of privatization, through which the transition from communism to capitalism was organized, was no less dialectical. The complete abolition of the private ownership of the means of production was seen by the theoreticians and practitioners of Soviet communism as the crucial precondition for constructing first a socialist and subsequently a communist society. Only the total state-socialization of all private property could bring about the total social plasticity necessary if the Communist Party were to obtain completely new and unparalleled formative power over society. The abolition of private property entailed a radical break with the past, and even with history as such, for this was understood as the history of private property relations. But above all, this abolition meant that art was granted precedence over nature – over human nature and over nature as such. If the 'natural rights' of humans, including the right to private property, are abolished, and their 'natural' bonds to their ancestry, their heritage and their 'innate' cultural tradition are also broken off, then humanity can invent itself anew and in complete freedom. Only the human who no longer possesses anything is freely available for every social experiment. The abolition of private property therefore represents the transition from the natural to the artificial, from the kingdom of necessity to the kingdom of (politically formative) freedom, from the traditional state to the total artwork.

On this basis, the re-introduction of private property forms an equally decisive precondition for ending the communist experiment, at least at first glance. The disappearance of a communist-governed state accordingly does not represent a merely political event. We know from history that governments, political systems and relations of power have often been altered without rights to private property being essentially affected. In these cases, social and economic life remains structured according to private law even as political life undergoes a radical transformation. By contrast, following the abdication of the Soviet Union there was no longer any social contract in force. Giant territories became abandoned and lawless wastelands, which, as in the period of the American Wild West, had to be newly structured. That is to say, they had to be parcelled out, distributed, and released for private appropriation – and in accordance with rules that were in fact dictated by the state leadership itself. Clearly, there is no possibility of completely returning by this route to a condition that existed prior to the state-socialization of goods, prior to the abolition of inheritance, prior to the break with the origin of private wealth.

Privatization ultimately proves to be just as artificial a political construct as socialization was before it. The same state that had once socialized in order to build communism now privatized in order to build capitalism. In both cases private property is equally subordinated to a *raison d'état*, and is thus manifestly an artefact, a product of a statecraft of deliberate planning. Privatization as the (re-)introduction of private property therefore does not lead back to nature – to natural inheritance and to natural law. Like its communist precursor, the postcommunist state is a constitutive and not merely an administrative power. Thus the postcommunist situation is distinguished by the fact that it reveals the artificiality of capitalism, in that it presents the emergence of capitalism as a purely political project of social reorganization, and not as the result of a 'natural' process of economic development.

The construction of capitalism in the Eastern European countries, pre-eminently in Russia, is not a consequence of economic or political necessity, nor an unavoidable and 'organic' historical transition. Rather, a political decision was taken to convert society from the construction of communism to the construction of capitalism, and to this end (and in complete accordance with classical Marxism) artificially to produce a class of private property owners in order to then make them the pillars of this construction. This involved the violent dismemberment and private appropriation of the dead body, the corpse of the socialist state, reminiscent of those bygone sacred feasts when members of a people or a tribe communally consumed the dead totemic animal. On the one hand, such a feast meant a privatization of the totemic animal, for each person received a little private piece of it; on the other hand, however, through precisely this privatization, these feasts formed the basis of the tribe's supra-individual and supra-private community. The materialist dialectic of the corpse here demonstrates its enduring effectiveness.

The real effrontery of Stalinist-style socialism consisted in its anti-utopianism, that is, in its assertion that utopia was basically already realized in the Soviet Union. The really existing place in which the socialist camp had been established was proclaimed to be the non-place of utopia. No special effort or insight is required – nor was any needed back then – to prove that this assertion is counterfactual, that the official idyll was manipulated by the state, and that conflict and struggle continued, whether as the struggle for individual survival, as the struggle against repression and manipulation, or as permanent revolution. And nonetheless, it is just as impossible to dismiss the famous claim 'it is done' from the world once and for all simply by referring to factual injustices and shortcomings, as it is to dispel the no less famous dogmas 'atman is brahman' or 'samsara is nirvana', for it involves a paradoxical identity of anti-utopia and utopia, hell and paradise, damnation and salvation. The no less paradoxical metanoia of re-privatization finally gave the event of communism its historical form. And with that, communism was in fact no longer utopia – its earthly incarnation was completed. Completed here means finished, and thus set free for repetition.

Such repetition certainly does not mean a return to Soviet communism, which is a historically unique and definitively concluded phenomenon. But further attempts to establish rule through language, that is to say, to establish the kingdom of philosophy, are very probable – indeed, are inevitable. Language is more universal and more democratic than money. It is, moreover, a more effective medium than money, for more can be said than can be bought and sold. But above all, the linguistification of social power relations gives to every individual human the possibility of contradicting power, fate and life – of criticizing them, accusing them, cursing them. Language is the medium of equality. When power becomes linguistic, it is compelled to operate under the conditions of the equality of all speakers – whether it wishes to or not. Admittedly, the equality of language is distorted and even destroyed if it is demanded that all speakers construct arguments of formal-logical validity. But the task of philosophy is precisely that of freeing humans from oppression by formal-logically valid language. Philosophy is a type of desire, for it is defined as the unfulfilled and unfulfillable love of wisdom. But it is a desire that has been totally linguistified, and its paradoxicality has thus been made transparent. Philosophy is an institution that offers humans the chance to live in self-contradiction without having to hide this fact. On this basis, the wish to expand this institution to the whole of society can never be wholly suppressed.